MW01633376

How to Try Again

ALSO BY STEVE KAMB

Level Up Your Life: How to Unlock Adventure and Happiness by Becoming the Hero of Your Own Story

How to Try Again

AN APPROACHABLE GUIDE TO
NAVIGATING CHAOS AND MAKING CHANGE THAT STICKS

STEVE KAMB

ST. MARTIN'S PRESS
NEW YORK

First published in the United States by St. Martin's Press, an imprint of St. Martin's Publishing Group

EU Representative: Macmillan Publishers Ireland Ltd, 1st Floor, The Liffey Trust Centre, 117–126 Sheriff Street Upper, Dublin 1, D01 YC43

www.stmartins.com

Designed by Gabriel Guma

The Library of Congress Cataloging-in-Publication Data is available upon request.

ISBN 978-1-250-34464-9 (hardcover)
ISBN 978-1-250-34465-6 (ebook)

First Edition: 2026

10 9 8 7 6 5 4 3 2 1

CONTENTS

INTRODUCTION

Starting at the End

I wonder why it is that when I plan a route too carefully it goes to pieces, whereas if I blunder along in blissful ignorance aimed in a fancied direction I get through with no trouble.

—John Steinbeck, *Travels with Charley: In Search of America*

Most books start at the beginning.

We're going to start at the end.

The morning after you failed. The day after you bailed on your diet. The week after you gave up on your 5K training. The month after you lost your job or your relationship fell apart. That moment when you're sad and frustrated and wondering, "Where do I go from here?"

I'll start with some uplifting news: You're in good company.

My name is Steve Kamb, and I have failed a lot lately.

The only reason you're reading this book is because of those failures.

In 2023, I signed a contract to write a book about how I've helped millions of busy, burned-out people reach their goals while living beautifully unoptimized lives. I was excited to share my seventeen years of experience teaching how to make progress even when life doesn't go according to plan.

And then *my* life didn't go according to plan.

Two weeks after signing this book deal, my dermatologist gave me the lovely news that the itchy patch on my scalp was basal cell carcinoma. "Don't worry, that's the good kind," she said. A surgery and some stitches took care of it this time, but I assume this will be the first of many skin cancer diagnoses in my future.

And then things really got "fun."

After a nine-year relationship, I got divorced.

I know divorce is quite common, particularly when shared life goals no longer overlap, but that didn't make mine hurt any less. Things ended amicably, but it still resulted in a shattered heart, fear around how my life would change, and the need to toss my perfectly crafted plan for the future right in the trash.

Even better, all of this happened at the same time my company fell apart.

Thanks to society-wide changes in how people use search engines, artificial intelligence, and social media, I watched as 75 percent of my company's website traffic—1.5 million monthly visitors—disappeared over just a few years.

I tried keeping my whole team together for as long as I could, but eventually I had to face reality. We went through a reckoning, a downsizing, and a company-wide reinvention for the tenth time. Admittedly, all of this happening while my personal life went through similar turmoil wasn't great.

Okay, it sucked.

Particularly because things usually just "work out" for me.

I'm lucky as hell. I was born on third base. I'm an overachieving people pleaser with workaholic tendencies. My solution to every problem has always been "just work harder." And for almost four decades, that (mostly) worked. I built a pretty great company and a pretty great life.

And then it all stopped working, all at the same time.

These past three years forced me to rethink my life. I had to change how I talked to myself. I had to let go of my expectations for the future. I had to forget any goal I had for my business. I had to adjust how I thought about solving problems.

I even had to redefine who I was as a person.

Here's the funniest part: This all happened *after* I signed the paperwork to write a book about how I help people navigate these same problems.

And even then, it still took me eighteen months to accept that the very skills I taught *other* people also applied to my situation. True statement: It was in draft number fourteen when I finally found the courage to add my personal failings to this introduction.

If you remember those old Hair Club for Men commercials, I'm going to hijack their slogan:

I'm not just the author of *How to Try Again,* I'm also a client.

I'm starting with the story of my life crashing down around me, not because I'm planning to say, "I got through some hard times, and so can you!" That's as cliché as it is untrue and unhelpful. I'm still figuring things out. I don't know what tomorrow will bring. I also don't know you personally, though I do know you have impeccable taste in reading material.

I also can't promise things will get better for either of us!

I'm not going to tell you that your failure is a blessing or that it's meant to be. While some failures end up being a benefit after the fact, we can't know that now. Sometimes, failure is just a crappy, unfair thing that catches us off guard. Sometimes life throws a sucker punch we never see coming.

So, where does that leave us?

I know you want things to be better. I do too. I bet you're also worried "better," whatever that means, is out of reach. You're probably tired of feeling stuck, and on the verge of giving up. You might even be thinking, "This is more proof life doesn't work out for people like me."

Fortunately, I wrote this book for people *like you*.

Who This Book Is for and Why I Wrote It

Some people wake up at 4 a.m., run fifteen miles barefoot, meditate in an ice bath, eat a breakfast of organic egg whites, drink a glass of unicorn tears, journal for an hour, and then write The Great American Novel.

This book is not for those people.

This book is for the rest of us.

Burned-out humans who are frustrated that they can't "get it together." Busy moms and dads who "*should* exercise more" or "*should* eat better" or "*should* be more productive." Folks with goals and hopes and dreams, but also have to live with pesky complications like jobs and kids and aging parents. People who struggle to implement popular strategies because their brains or bodies work differently. Mortals who look at all the hustle culture and photoshopped influencers on social media and think, "I have absolutely nothing in common with these people."

If any of that sounds like you, you've come to the right place.

Although talking about my success makes me even more uncomfortable than talking about my failures, I'm pretty good at this stuff and have been doing it for a long time. So, thanks for letting me awkwardly brag for the next two paragraphs.

Tens of millions of readers and a worldwide community have popped up around my writing at NerdFitness.com, a company I started in 2009. You've maybe even stumbled across one of my one thousand fitness or nutrition articles with fun LEGO photos. We've hosted legendary live events like Camp Nerd Fitness (with hundreds of campers flying in from all over the globe), half a dozen people have Nerd Fitness tattoos, and more than a few relationships have begun in our online community, "The Rebellion." I've given talks at some of the world's biggest companies and our story has been featured in publications like the *The Wall Street Journal* and *The Washington Post.*

We also have an unbelievable team of coaches that have helped tens of thousands of people get their first pull-up, run their first 5K, transform themselves physically and mentally, and finally build sustainable habits. We help people of all shapes, sizes, and life experiences build flexible, resilient lives.

And we do so differently from what you might expect.

Rather than helping people succeed with more discipline, we help them fail with more compassion.

Instead of simply building a perfect workout program to follow, we help clients get back on track after a sick dog causes them to miss a week. Instead of shaming people for eating fast food with their kids, we help them fit fast food into their flexible weekly plan. Instead of chasing temporary changes for temporary results, we help our audience make sustainable progress with sustainable results.

We help real people navigate real problems better than anybody else in the galaxy. We've been doing this at a high level for a long time and we have helped a lot of people succeed after years (or decades) of struggling.

This book is the culmination of my work and my team's expertise.

How This Book Will Help You Try Again

Change is really, really hard.

Of course running a marathon is hard: It's so far!

Of course writing a book is hard: It's so many words!

Of course meditating is hard: Being alone with our thoughts is terrifying!

We're trying to make long-term changes (boring) without instant gratification (lame) while being surrounded by unlimited food, dopamine, and amazing technology (fun) that keeps us complacent, overstimulated, and distracted (party).

No wonder we struggle to follow through on our goals. We need a different approach. One that factors in what life is actually like. One that honors the reality that we're fallible humans trying to make arbitrary changes, with a brain that hates change, and a world that wants to keep us where we are: perpetually dissatisfied and hungry for the next quick fix.

It's called *How to Try Again* because it's not just "trying again" that matters, but *how* we try again that makes all the difference.

No matter what goal or habit or change we're trying to follow through on, human nature and Mother Nature will do whatever possible to get in the way.

We're going to do things differently this time. I promise not to use any motivational platitudes like "Winners never quit!" or "Failure is not an option!" First of all, winners quit all the time, and failure is sometimes the *best* option.

I also have a nit to pick with the world's most famous quote on resilience: "If at first you don't succeed, try, try again."

Maybe! But probably not.

What if we're trying to succeed at the wrong thing?

Maybe our expectations for "success" are completely unrealistic?

If we just "try, try again," won't we just "fail, fail again?"

Doing the same thing over and over again and expecting different results is, well, the definition of insanity.

Maybe we need to accept that something needs to change.

Perhaps we need to reset our expectations and ask for help. Maybe we need to realize we're worthy of putting ourselves first every once in a while.

We're going to cover all of this in this book.

I don't promise to have all the answers. Nobody does.

Here's what I can promise: empathy, plenty of bad jokes, and a different path that *might* work. A new philosophy that treats failure compassionately and success differently.

And a step-by-step blueprint for navigating chaos.

How This Book Is Organized

We'll start by diving into whatever failure we're currently struggling with. The problem is *not* that we failed. It's that our relationship with failure needs to be mended. What we're trying to avoid is a situation where we follow the words of the philosopher Homer (Simpson): "You tried, and you failed miserably. The lesson is 'Never try.'"

Luckily, we'll cover that right away in our first chapter:

- **Chapter 1:** The Unexpected Benefits of Failure

We'll reframe how we view failure and how we talk to ourselves about our failures. If you wake up every day feeling like a failure because you haven't done "enough," or that you can't start living until reaching your goals, I got you covered.

We'll then move on to the foundational framework of our book: making a PACT.

PART ONE: LET'S MAKE A PACT

Once we've forgiven ourselves for being human, and made peace with whatever past failures or challenges we've faced, we can then get to work on what to do next.

And that's when we're going to "make a PACT."[1]

No, this isn't a proprietary, double-secret protocol. It's not the "one true path" to health, wellness, and productivity Nirvana. It's not magic, nor will it solve every problem.

Rather than a set-in-stone rule, PACT is a foundational framework that lets you be "pretty good, most of the time."

Just like on *Sesame Street*, each letter stands for a word and a chapter of our book:

- **Chapter 2:** P Is for Pause: How to Not Make Things Worse
- **Chapter 3:** A Is for Accept: Why "Normal" Isn't Normal, and That's Normal

---

1 I'd be remiss if I didn't point out that in Dungeons & Dragons terms, Warlocks make PACTs with all-powerful beings. If you don't currently have access to a demi-god, Cthulhu, or the Flying Spaghetti Monster, making a PACT with yourself is the next best thing.

- **Chapter 4:** C Is for Change: What's Different This Time?
- **Chapter 5:** T Is for Try: Start Ugly and Get Good

When life throws a curveball, we pause and accept. We shift expectations, change, and charge ahead. And we can literally repeat the PACT framework until the heat death of the universe, the Robot Apocalypse, or our brains get uploaded into the cloud.

PART TWO: HOW TO USE PACTS IN OUR LIVES

Once we've done the hard work of building the PACT framework, it's time to take it out for a test drive!

We'll treat the second half of this book like a Choose Your Own Adventure novel, depending on where you're at on your next attempt. We'll cover what to try next and how to give that next attempt the best possible chance to succeed. I'll not only teach you how to keep doing "the thing" but also how our brains will sabotage us along the way (brains are fun, aren't they?).

Then there's going to come a time when life decides to totally kick your ass in the most unfair way possible. Fortunately, I've got you covered for that situation too. And finally we'll see what life can look like when we stack our PACTs one after another.

- **Chapter 6:** How to Pick the Next Thing to Try
- **Chapter 7:** Escape the Doom Loop: How to Protect Yourself from Yourself
- **Chapter 8:** How to Keep Doing the Thing
- **Chapter 9:** When Life Kicks Your Ass, Here's What to Do
- **Chapter 10:** How to Navigate Life with Flexible Resilience

Each chapter is full of stories you'll remember, built around a PACT framework you'll never forget. If you can apply these lessons, they can help with not only navigating an unpredictable life, but building a healthier relationship with yourself too.

We're going to transform our lives together, and we're going to do it while still managing to get the stuff done that needs to get done.

Everybody wins!

While we live in a world full of performative productivity hacks ("Rise and grind!") and apathetic nihilism ("Who cares, none of this matters!"), this book will have you saying, "Thanks, Steve! I now have the skills and mindset to become a massive failure!"

That came out wrong, but you know what I mean.

This is my life's work, and I can't wait to share it with you.

1

THE UNEXPECTED BENEFITS OF FAILURE

We Are Not Failures. We're Humans Who Failed at Something.

I've made a huge mistake.

—G.O.B. Bluth, *Arrested Development*

I have fantastic news: We're not that special.

Failure, shame, and dissatisfaction have played an outsized role in the human condition since the beginning of time. Which makes sense, because for 99.9 percent of our existence, life has been brutal and failure has frequently meant death.

Twelve thousand years ago, if poor Bonk the caveman slept through his alarm clock (the actual sun), he missed the morning hunt with his fellow warriors. This failure got him ostracized from his tribe, which probably resulted in his death from disease or a mountain lion.

Five hundred-ish generations later, we are the anxious descendants of those failure-avoidant humans who survived. Although we now work in (hopefully) safe environments, can order food with our phones, and are chasing arbitrary goals, our brains still operate like the cave-people days. They tell us, "I avoided that scary situation and I'm not dead. Being cautious has kept me alive 100 percent of the time."

I'm generalizing, and much has been written on the topic, but the point is this: Failure, shame, and the fear of failure take up a disproportionate amount of space in our lives.

No wonder, as Rick Hanson points out in *Buddha's Brain*:

"Our brain is like Velcro for negative experiences but Teflon for positive ones."

There's even a scientific term for this: the negativity bias. We get "sticky brain" and dwell on the bad things that (might) happen, and so easily ignore all the good things that happen. It's a survival mechanism at work.

Fortunately, reality paints a different picture. Unless our failure was preceded by "Hold my beer and watch this," it probably didn't kill us. It's something that happened (or happened to us). Our cave-people brains have chosen to interpret it in a certain way. It's a feeling that's within our head and felt within our body.

And yeah, of course failure hurts.

Particularly if our failure was public, career-altering, or involved other people. Personally, I opted for all the failures, all at once, which I wouldn't recommend. Being seen failing sucks, and shame is a really powerful negative emotion.

But failure isn't a life sentence. Shame does not mean the end for us. It's not a permanent addition to our identity.

We are not failures.

We are humans who failed at something.

We are so much more than our failures. Any one failure is simply a part of the totality of the life that we've lived. It's just unfortunate that it's become something that sticks like glue to our identity. It wasn't always this way.

Using the word "failure" to describe a person is a relatively new construct. As author Scott Sandage points out in *Born Losers,* "early Americans 'made' failures, but it took a while before failures made—or unmade—men."

In 1828, Noah Webster defined failure as "a breaking, or becoming insolvent" in his dictionary (yes, that Webster's dictionary!). A failure was something that happened.

But over the rest of the nineteenth century, things changed as society changed and industry changed. The "self-made man" and ambition became the prevailing attitude for life in America. People started getting labeled as failures for lacking ambition or struggling in life. Webster died in 1843, but his dictionary continued, and a revised edition in 1857 redefined failure as "some weakness in a man's character, disposition, or habit." Failure had become a character flaw and moral shortcoming.

Unfortunately, that altered definition is the one that stuck. Which brings us to today.

Depending on what we've failed at or how stuck we feel, we might think we're lost causes, that our failures and shortcomings are uniquely our own. That we must wear a scarlet "F" on our shirt and carry our shame everywhere. That we *are* failures.

It's time to turn back the clock to Webster's original definition.

We may have failed. Not because we're flawed, but because

failure is the most common of all human experiences, outside of breathing and complaining about traffic.

We just never talk about it, because shame and guilt are such powerful emotions.

Fortunately, the tide is turning.

Talking about our failures is no longer something to avoid. There's now a museum dedicated to some of the most epic fails in history and a college class that teaches students to embrace failure.

Failure Is One Possible Outcome of Anything Worth Doing

In 2023, I took a trip to the Museum of Failure, a touring museum created by psychologist Dr. Samuel West.

It was packed full of history's most famous failures, flops, and frauds. Proudly on display was the Hula Chair: a swiveling seat designed to allegedly help people shed stubborn belly fat by doing a sitting "hula dance." Instead, it tosses the victim's body and torso around like a medieval torture device.

Would not recommend.

There was a model of the Swedish king Gustav II's comically expensive military warship. After years of delays and dozens of nonsensical alterations, it sank to the bottom of the harbor fifty minutes into its celebratory voyage. Talk about a sunk cost. (Don't worry, the bad jokes in this book are going to get much worse.)

The museum also featured a model plane and the absurd tale of Hooters Air. Yes, *that* Hooters. If you ever feel like a failure for not making smarter decisions, just imagine *how many people* had to agree with the following sentence: "We got rich making chicken wings; how hard could it be to run a profitable airline?"

I assume Hooters Seminary School and Hooters Brain Surgery Academy were the next two ideas on the list.

Now, alongside these obvious disasters, I found failed products from some of the world's most successful companies. My beloved Nintendo had quite a few on display: Even my mom and dad knew not to buy me the Nintendo Virtual Boy, a 1995 headset that could cause eye strain for some children and was discontinued by 1996. Oops!

Microsoft was well represented too, most notably with their ill-fated Zune MP3 player. It was supposed to take down the iPod and instead ended up forgotten.

Even Apple, one of the most successful companies in history, had a video game console on display called the Pippin. This console was so unsuccessful that even I, a proud nerd gamer, had never heard of it.

In addition to the clear failures and terrible ideas, there were many featured products that were casualties of poor timing: early chatbots, multifunctional cell phones, personal digital assistants, and the first digital camera, invented in the mid-1970s. It was such a breakthrough that Kodak never released it for fear of cannibalizing their sales of physical film! (We know how that worked out for them in the long term: They filed for bankruptcy in 2012.)

For so many of these failures, they were just too early. The vision was there, and once technology finally caught up to the ambition, the road had been paved for companies to have far grander and more important successes down the road.

The more failures I saw, the more I came to understand failure differently. This museum didn't only exist to poke fun at bad inventions. I mean sure, it did that too. I'm still laughing about Hooters Air. But it also showed the ways in which failure was simply the cost of doing business. Spending the afternoon in the museum reshaped how I thought about setbacks, risk, and the opportunity cost of living in fear of failure.

Failure isn't a flaw that must be prevented from happening. So many rewards in life are only available to those willing to open themselves up to failure as a possibility.

Dr. Theresa MacPhail (yes, she has the perfect last name), an associate professor of science and technology studies at Stevens University, observed that many overachieving college students struggle to handle their first academic failures. She knew this wouldn't be the last adversity they'd face in their lives, so she decided to do something about it. In addition to her classes, she took a chance and offered to teach a class on embracing and reframing failure. In the greatest of ironies, her class has become so successful that seven years later, it has a long waitlist every semester.

And until we can sneak into Dr. MacPhail's class, let's see what lessons failure can teach us. Here are the most important.

Failure is one possible outcome for anything worth doing.

Ed Catmull, one of the founders of the animation studio Pixar, said it best in the book *Creativity, Inc.*: "Failure isn't a necessary evil. In fact, it isn't evil at all. It is a necessary consequence of doing something new."

It's why Pixar encourages their teams to embrace these counterintuitive strategies:

- It's not a manager's responsibility to avoid risks, but to make it safe for the team to take more risks.
- The cost of preventing mistakes is often far greater than the cost of fixing them.
- The job isn't to protect against change or uncertainty, but to develop the ability to recover after unexpected events occur.

If failure is one possible outcome, then adding extra pressure and shame on top of failure isn't serving us.

It's not something to be avoided nor something to be ashamed of. Let's return once again to the Museum of Failure, where its final exhibit changed my feelings on shame and failure forever.

Failure Connects Us All. Let's Talk About It.

If you've failed or sabotaged yourself at some point, you're in good company.

We've done this song and dance for so long the ancient Greeks even had a term for it. "Akrasia" means "acting against one's better judgment."[2]

If the ancient Greeks had a word for it, we can take solace in the fact that we're not doing anything out of the ordinary or uncommon to the human experience when we mess up.

And this is where the Museum of Failure really shines. After a few hours of exploring, I walked toward the exit and stumbled upon the most important exhibit of all: a wall of multicolored Post-it notes from guests who had written out their deepest, most personal failures.

It was a kaleidoscope of a thousand notes, each a declaration from somebody who "screwed up."

One read "Three failed start-ups," while another lamented "Two failed marriages." "I failed nursing school" was sandwiched between "Not finishing my bachelor's degree" and "Tried to cut my own bangs."

"I farted in yoga" was the most honest sticky note on that board, though that's less relevant to the point I'm trying to make here. I just thought it was worth pointing out, in case you're the person who left that note. I salute you, yoga farter.[3]

This "wall of failure" exposed the depths of the collective human struggle in a way that was surprisingly uplifting.

Not because I wanted to wallow in others' misery, or because

---

2 The ancient Greeks also had a term, "callipygous," which means "having beautiful buttocks," which I thought bared mentioning. (Cough.)

3 Please contact me if you were the one who wrote this!

it made me say, "Could be worse." Hearing about other people's failures helped me realize I wasn't alone. And boy, have I needed this reminder lately.

When we suffer in silence with failure, it has a way of growing and growing in our minds. It lies to us about how bad we are, and how much additional torture we must put ourselves through. None of this is true. But that's not apparent until we share our failures with others, and we realize we've all failed at something.

Many failures are outside of our control. Others are because we made a very human mistake or didn't show up as our best self. It happens. Connecting with others who have also failed is an amazing way to remember we're all in this together.

I've thought a lot about the "wall of failure" lately.

It has helped quiet the voice in my head that told me my failures were identity-defining. That nobody had ever gone through what I was going through. That I deserved the guilt and shame I found myself wallowing in, simply because parts of my life didn't go according to plan.

It turns out I'm not that unique.

Not only were my failures common, but there were thousands of people who had gone through similar challenges. After waiting for eighteen months to heal (and also partly out of shame), I shared an update about the end of my marriage and my business struggles in a newsletter. The response was overwhelming and overflowing with support. Many readers thanked me for giving them the courage to share their own.

Like the museum's Post-it notes, each reply made me feel more connected with my fellow human disasters who had failed in similar ways and offered advice if they were further along in their journey. I was moved to tears.

This changed my perspective and gave me the courage to share my story in this book. Failures shouldn't be kept private or hidden in shame. When we talk about them, it can take away the power they have over us.

We are human, therefore we will fail. A lot. We might as well talk about it.

Sharing our failures with others isn't just a cathartic release of shame. It's a badge of honor that shows "I was brave enough to try something." Perhaps most important, sharing our failure might help somebody else who is currently destroying themselves silently for their own failure.

No matter how badly you've failed, or whatever flaw you're

currently beating yourself up for, I want you to know you're not alone. You're part of a nonexclusive club: forgivable humans who try things and fail often.

There are hundreds of thousands of years of history with billions of people who have failed at similar things as you and me. Whether it's a failed workout or a failed diet, a failed business or a failed relationship, it's definitive proof that we are human, part of an unbroken lineage of fellow weirdos, held together with spit and duct tape. Although our failures might feel like they're uniquely our own, talking about them with our friends will reveal a universal truth: We're all struggling, we've all failed, and we're all in this together.

So, wherever you're at in your current struggle, you are right where you need to be.

Not because you're beyond repair.

But because you're human.

Welcome to the club.

There are eight-billion-plus of us.

Why We Never Start Back at Square One

It's now time to thank our past selves for failing at something. Here's a common example. Let's say we signed up for a gym membership a year ago.

We went a few times, life happened, and we bailed. We're demoralized that we've gone all the way back to "square one" on our fitness journey. We feel like a failure because we're "starting over."

Fortunately, we get to bring all of our past knowledge with us, because we've already taken so many difficult steps.

After all, going to the gym isn't *one* decision.

It's multiple decisions.

We had to first decide to join a gym and then research which one to join.

Then we had to find the gym, figure out the pricing, and sign up.

Then we had to drive and find parking.

Then we had to motivate ourselves to walk through the front door.

Then we had to learn where the locker room was, where to fill up our water bottle, and where to change into our workout clothes.

Then we had to learn how the machines or treadmill work and find enough courage to exercise in public.

No wonder they say the heaviest weight in the gym is the front door. And we had to try and do all of this within the confines of our busy life. Just getting to "I went to the gym" takes a ton of mental bandwidth, effort, and courage.

So, when we're ready to try again, no matter how far back we've fallen, we never start over at Square One.

We know where the gym is. We know where to park. We know how the equipment works. We know what to wear. We've already learned the toughest parts.

Sure, we might be starting over with how much we can lift on the bar or how fast we can walk or jog. But we already have the knowledge from every past attempt and will quickly move through the early steps. It's like learning to ride a bike: Once we've done it, quite a bit of that knowledge and muscle memory stays with us.

Not only that, but our hard-earned knowledge might help us avoid the pitfalls we fell into last time. We can then use our precious and limited energy to make it even further on this attempt. When viewed through this lens, each failure is not a step backward, but a step forward.

We get to bring the experience of every past attempt with us, and that knowledge might be the difference maker on our next attempt.

This idea that "knowledge gained through failure is progress" is the premise of one of my favorite video games. *Outer Wilds*, by Mobius Digital, is a game without levels, experience points, or weapons. There's no resource gathering or base building. There are no enemies or boss battles.

The main character is an astronaut caught in a twenty-two-minute time loop, trying to solve the mystery of an exploding sun in a tiny solar system. Think *Groundhog Day* meets *Interstellar.* My experience with *Outer Wilds* included dozens upon dozens of deaths, most of them *hilarious.* I flew my spaceship directly into the sun. I crashed into the moon going 300 miles per hour. I punctured my spacesuit on a cactus. I got sucked into a black hole. And if I survived long enough, the sun would explode. After each death, I'd wake up at the beginning, with only the knowledge of what *not* to do.

What begins as a confusing exploration of planets in a solar system becomes an addictive loop of iteration, experimentation, and progress through failure. By the end of the game, after twenty-plus hours of comical deaths, the mystery is solved within a single twenty-two-minute loop, thanks only to the knowledge gained along the way.

What a beautiful metaphor for life.

We stand on the shoulders of Past Us.

We not only need to thank our past failures for getting us here, but we can be proud of them. They made us who we are and taught us everything we know. Maybe it took us longer to learn some lessons than others, but I think that's okay too.

We get to bring all that knowledge with us.

That means there's hope for us yet.

Failure isn't the end, but the beginning.

Failure Is the First Step, Not the Last

Singer-songwriter (and national treasure) Dolly Parton once said, "I thank God for my failures. Maybe not at the time, but after some reflection. I never feel like a failure just because something I tried has failed."

If failure is good enough for Dolly, then maybe it's good enough for us too.

The broken bone is a sign we tried a new activity. The once-used treadmill in the corner means we had hope and started on a change. The bag of unopened spring mix in our vegetable drawer means we were *so close* to actually making a salad this time. The end of a relationship means that we loved and were loved.

The only true failure is when we let our past experiences prevent future attempts altogether.

Giving up on a fad diet two years ago doesn't mean we're doomed to struggle with our relationship with food forever. Writing a book that's bombed doesn't mean the next book couldn't become a breakout success. The end of a relationship doesn't mean we're incompatible with love, nor does it mean we'll never love again.

Our future progress is waiting behind our current failures.

Each failure is the first step on a new path.

In fact, it *can* be the very thing we look back on and say, "I'm actually glad that happened." Of course, we don't need to feel bad if we're not "grateful" for failing. I'm not here to gloss things over; failure can still totally suck sometimes.

But it can also be a catalyst for changes we're proud of.

We don't need to figure all of that out right now. We can just let failure be a thing that happened, and decide where to go from here. As Jean Craighead George wrote in *My Side of the Mountain*: "The sun has a wonderfully glorious habit of rising every morning."

You're here reading this.

Which means you woke up today.

That's a good start.

We can build on that.

Today doesn't need to be a day to make a dramatic declaration, or draw up a new life plan. It doesn't have to be a day for judgment or surrendering or tormenting ourselves, nor a day to say "Look on the bright side."

It can be a day where we forgive ourselves for being human.

A human that's part of an unbroken line of forgivable mortals who survived long enough to get you here, reading this book today. A human who's not alone.

Speaking of which, if you want to feel less alone, visit HowToTryAgain.com/Fail where you can see the failures of other readers who were brave enough to share. If you're up for it, add your own!

Sharing our failures can help take away some of their power, and might help somebody else navigate their own struggles. More important, connecting to a larger group of humans who have also failed can remind us that we're all in this together and that our failures got us here.

We've survived one hundred percent of our failures so far. I like our chances for what's coming next.

Let's make a PACT and get started.

Key Insights

Failure scares us, because we're still wired for "Failure means death." Ten thousand years ago, failure often meant death by animal or accident or ostracization. We're no longer in danger all day every day, but our brains often still *feel* like we are.

We aren't failures. We're humans who failed at something. Our brains love to overidentify with our failures and attach them to our egos. We *feel* like a failure, when the reality is that we are humans who failed at something. That's it. Sometimes it's our fault, and oftentimes it isn't. We can put some distance between us and the action. We're humans; therefore, we fail.

Failure is one possible outcome for anything worth doing. Whenever we feel embarassment or shame about a failure, we can remember there's a whole Museum of Failure that shows some of the world's worst inventions and ideas that were far too early. Failure is the cost of doing business, and shows that we tried. Failure can be celebrated. Even if that failure was Hooters Air.

Don't suffer in silence. Share your failure. When we share our failures with others, it can take their power away, and help us realize that our problems are not particularly unique or unsolvable. They connect all of us in this wonderfully chaotic experiment that is the human race. Visit HowToTryAgain.com/fail.

Remember, there's no Square One. No matter how far we think we have to go or how many times we've failed, we get to stand on the shoulders of every past attempt we've made. This is amazing! "Starting over" includes all the hard-earned knowledge from our past, which means we can catch back up quickly.

Failure is the first step, not the last. We've failed before; we'll fail again. Sharing our failures, and accepting that our failures do not define us, is a great place to start. All future success is trapped behind our current struggle, so the only real failure is when we stop trying.

Part One

LET'S MAKE A PACT

Now that we've reframed our relationship with failure, let's get to work on trying again. We're going to do this by following a simple framework that spells out PACT:

- **P**ause
- **A**ccept
- **C**hange
- **T**ry

When life feels out of control, when we feel like we're drowning, when we're weighed down by shame or guilt about not being further along, we can embrace the PACT.

We'll spend a chapter on each letter, and show how to implement each element in our own lives:

- In **Chapter 2: P Is for Pause**, we'll learn how to NOT panic or make things worse, and then how to deploy an effective strategy when we feel like we're drowning.

- In **Chapter 3: A Is for Accept**, we'll learn why the word "normal" is misunderstood, the difference between "giving up" and quitting, and how to embrace "Yes, and" thinking.
- In **Chapter 4: C Is for Change**, we'll study two unlikely professions to modify how we think about change: grizzled detectives and curious scientists.
- In **Chapter 5: T Is for Try**, we'll dissect the most important word in this book: "try." We'll "start ugly," learn the art of hilarious improvement, and "get good."

THE PACT FRAMEWORK

Pause

Accept

Change

Try

2

P IS FOR PAUSE

How to Not Make Things Worse

There is no problem so bad that you can't make it worse.

—Astronaut Chris Hadfield

It's time for the first step of the PACT.

You might think I'm going to tell you to get back on the horse. To pick yourself up and get back to work. That would make sense. When we think about making changes in our life and moving toward a goal, the first word we think of is "progress."

And boy, do we humans love progress.

It makes us feel good.

Progress means we're improving our lot in life. We want to see the number in our bank account go up, the number of pages written on our manuscript increase, or the amount of weight we lift get heavier. Seeing positive movement toward a goal gives us that warm, fuzzy feeling and a sense of control that we are making things better.

And when we are NOT making progress? We feel like we're falling behind.

When we don't see the number on the scale change, when we're not getting stronger, or when we aren't advancing in our career, it can be demoralizing. We feel "stuck."

However, there's an important third option we're not considering.

The opposite of progress isn't stagnation or staying where we are.

It's "regress."

Moving backward. Away from our goal.

Making sh** worse, essentially.

When we find ourselves struggling to make progress, our inclination is to *try again, but harder.* As you'll soon learn, trying again or working harder *might* be the wrong move, and we might be making things worse.

When compared to this path, "not making progress" can actually be the best, most optimal decision right now.

How to Not Make Things Worse

We're going to kick things off with a story about the worst vacation ever.

At least, for the guy who lived to tell the tale.

In 2013, Brett Archibald and his childhood friends from South Africa reunited for a fiftieth-birthday surfing trip off the coast of Sumatra, Indonesia. What was supposed to be a celebration turned into a horror movie. While boating between Sumatra and the Mentawai Islands, Brett woke up in the middle of the night suffering from food poisoning.

He went to the top deck of the boat to vomit up his dinner, and due to the rough seas, Brett fell 19 feet over the railing into the ocean. Uh-oh. He then got sucked under the boat and finally popped above the surface as the boat sailed away.

At this point it was 2 a.m., so Brett yelled, but failed to alert anybody. He soon found himself completely alone, floating in the Indian Ocean, dehydrated, with nobody aware that he had fallen overboard. I can't think of a more nightmarish scenario.

After realizing the boat wasn't coming back, he did the thing that we all would do in this situation: He picked an arbitrary direction and started swimming.

Pull, kick, breathe.

Pull, kick, breathe.

Pull, kick, breathe.

And this is how things continued for hours. As the sun started to brighten the early-morning sky, Brett still couldn't see any sign of a ship or land, so he took stock of everything he had on him.

Rummaging through his pockets, he found the little paper keycard holder from his hotel stay the night before. Knowing that ocean currents are powerful and can often lead toward land, he ripped off a tiny corner and placed it on top of the water.

He then watched as that tiny bit of paper floated away . . . in the opposite direction.

Brett had done what he thought he *should* do, only to discover he was making things worse. Not only was he swimming against the current and getting farther away from land, but he was burning precious energy at the same time. As soon as he realized this, he stopped swimming and started treading water.

We'll return to the unlikely conclusion of this story shortly, but let's explore this part of Brett's adventure first and the life lesson staring us in the face.

After something hasn't worked, it's human nature to try again, but say "I'll try harder this time." Unfortunately, trying harder while moving in the wrong direction is making things worse.

It's kind of like trying to run UP a down escalator, like I used to do as a kid at Filene's Basement while my mom shopped for shoes.

***Trying harder* at the same thing that already didn't work wastes energy that we can use to figure out a better solution.**

So, how do we know if we're on the wrong path? We need to pause long enough to ask the uncomfortable question "Is this actually working?"

If we've sent a hundred job applications with no interviews, sending a hundred more identical resumes into the void won't help. Instead, we can look up job fairs, reach out to friends, or have a mentor evaluate our resume.

If we've swiped right on a dating app a thousand times without a match, is swiping right a thousand more times going to help? Unlikely. Maybe a trusted friend can take a look at our dating profile, we can try new photos, or we could skip the apps entirely and go to a hiking meetup in our town.

If we've tried to follow the keto diet and given up every time Jan from accounting brings in doughnuts, is *trying harder* to go keto a good use of our limited willpower? Maybe there's a different strategy that doesn't make us miserable and allows room for the occasional treat.

By the way, don't worry. We all do this. There's comfort in continuing to do the same thing, even though it's not really working. Change is hard.

It's tough to admit the strategy we picked wasn't right for us, and all our effort was spent on the wrong thing.

Luckily, we know that no failure is wasted effort. It's a hard-earned lesson that teaches us what hasn't worked. Author C. S. Lewis spells out our next step clearly. "We all want progress, but if you're on the wrong road, progress means doing an about-turn and walking back to the right road; in that case, the man who turns back soonest is the most progressive man."

As soon as we realize we're chasing the wrong goal, as soon as we discover we're swimming against the current, the next correct step is to stop making things worse.

We need to pause, conserve energy, and process what's actually going on. This gives us a chance to eventually find a path or current that's headed in the right direction.

And the truth is, sometimes that next path might take a long time for us to find.

So, when our brain is telling us to "do more of the same thing that's not working," we can take a few minutes to pause and turn off autopilot. We can make sure we're not making things worse, and narrow our focus to staying afloat long enough to see what tomorrow brings.

The Art of Treading Water: Do Less to Stay Afloat Longer

Back to our guy Brett, floating in the Indian Ocean with absolutely nothing to see, in any direction, for hours upon hours.

Once he realized he was wasting energy furiously fighting the current, he stopped trying to swim somewhere, stopped making things worse, and just focused on doing the bare minimum to stay alive. Instead of asking, "When will I get rescued?" he asked, "What do I need to do right now to keep my head above the water?" And that's precisely what he did.

He stayed afloat.

He also had plenty to keep him busy: He was stung by a Portuguese man-o-war, dive-bombed by jerk birds, nibbled by a curious shark, and chomped relentlessly by tiny fish attracted to his chafed skin. I told you this was the worst vacation ever.

Through all of this, Brett kept treading water.

And early in the morning on April 18, twenty-eight hours later, his luck finally changed. While focusing on staying off the bottom of the ocean, he noticed a little red cross on the horizon. As the cross got bigger, he realized it was the mast of a boat heading in his direction. He yelled at the top of his lungs, managed to catch their attention, and was rescued 50 nautical miles away from where he had fallen off his boat.

Even more wild, it wasn't his boat that found him, but another charter boat that abandoned their own trip to go search for Brett while he was lost at sea.

After I picked my jaw up off the ground, I thought to myself, "How long can humans tread water for?"

It turns out, quite a long time.

In 1980, Albert Rizzo set the world record for treading water in the open sea with a time of 72 hours and 3 minutes.[4] Had you decided to tread water for this long, you could watch all seventy-three episodes of *Game of Thrones* and still have time to watch *The Breakfast Club* as a palate cleanser.

It turns out we humans are capable of more than you'd expect when it comes to staying afloat. Particularly if we narrow our focus to just doing the bare minimum for as long as possible.

Allowing ourselves to do *less* is more than just okay.

It can be life-preserving (pun definitely intended).

There might be areas of life in which we need to give ourselves permission to tread water and do less. Baby boomers might call it "coasting." Gen Z rebranded it as "quiet quitting." As a former gifted child who became an insecure overachiever, I call it "recovering from existential burnout."

This is also the main plot point of the 1999 movie classic *Of-*

4 Rizzo would go on to break his own record in the summer of 1983 by treading water for 108 hours, and then again in 1984 by treading water for 132 hours, until Guinness stopped tracking this world record.

fice Space. As I quoted in my high school graduation speech, the main character Peter Gibbons explains his lack of work ethic to Bob and Bob, the efficiency consultants: "It's not that I'm lazy, it's that I just don't care."

We can all probably channel more Peter Gibbons energy in our lives.

Maybe it's okay that we're not overachieving right now.

Maybe it's okay to let a few things go sideways while caring for an aging parent with dementia?

Maybe it's okay to strategically "coast" on parts of life while fostering a new rescue puppy.

Here's the fun part:

Doing less doesn't have to feel bad. Doing less can feel *good*.

The less we expect ourselves to do *all the things*, the more energy we can devote to staying afloat on the few things that really matter to us. When we feel weighed down with the pressure that we're so far behind or that we're not doing enough, we can pause. We can give ourselves a tiny bit of grace. Life is hard, we're asking too much of ourselves right now, and we're doing our best.

Instead of trying (and failing) to get better at juggling chainsaws, we can decide that maybe—just maybe—putting down the chainsaws is okay for now.

I remember having a conversation with my friend Eric Ruiz, who had just become a new dad; he was lamenting he only had time to do a handful of push-ups in the morning before his baby woke up and he started his work commute.

Rather than giving him more tactics to sneak in an optimized morning or telling him to wake up sooner to get in a full workout, I said, "It sounds like you're being a good dad, and it sounds like a few push-ups and squats is a full workout for you right now. That's amazing." I could see the tension in his shoulders receding, and the exercise guilt he felt for not doing more starting to fade.

When we find ourselves in the middle of a challenging situation, treading water can be more than enough.

Stop Trying to Win. Don't Lose.

When we think of change in "all-or-nothing" terms, we quickly go from "all" to "nothing" as soon as life gets in the way. Right now, as we're treading water, our only goal should be to "not lose."

In life, "losing" is when we throw in the towel, say "Screw it," and give up on everything because we're so overwhelmed. But if we give up now, it just makes everything more difficult for our future selves.

We need to stay in the fight. As economist Nassim Taleb says in his book *Antifragile*, "Chess grandmasters usually win by not losing; people become rich by not going bust (particularly when others do)."

Instead of furiously trying (and failing) to do all the things and burning out, we can stop trying to win and just focus on not losing. Instead of worrying about how much farther we have to go on a goal, or how far behind we feel, we can ask, "What needs to happen today to show I haven't given up yet?"

Once we accept that we're not capable of doing everything and making progress on all our goals at the same time, it gives us permission to strategically coast and set aside a few goals for now.

If we're dealing with a new routine because our young children are out of school for the summer, doing the bare minimum elsewhere is okay.

If we just moved and started a new job, letting our house get a bit messy and ordering more takeout meals than usual is perfectly acceptable.

We can give ourselves permission to "not lose," without expectation of progress or things getting better in the near future. We probably have too high an expectation for what we can handle right now anyway.

This is where treading water can be enough for us right now.

- *One* healthy meal per day can be enough to keep us from going off the rails for the next month.
- A ten-minute walk can be enough to keep us from staying glued to the couch for weeks.
- Some push-ups and squats can be enough to keep us from giving up for the next year.

Sometimes, "half-assed" is the most we can give.

That's great.

While writing this book and navigating the changes in my personal life, I needed to tread water mentally and physically. Instead of beating myself up for being behind, I set new baselines for everything. I shrank every expectation I had for my workouts, my professional goals, and what I thought my life *should* be. I asked myself what I could cut out, where I could scale back, and which expectations I could get rid of. I allowed myself to ask for help and to actually say no to requests.

I did the bare minimum to remind myself, "I haven't given up!"

Some days, that was a five-minute walk. Other days, it was one set of squats or pull-ups. Another day, it was choosing the grilled chicken strips instead of fried chicken nuggets at the airport. I had compassion for myself navigating a new reality.

My timeline was no longer measured in months or years. I was just trying to get to the next week. Sometimes, I was trying to get to the next day. Not because I assumed things would *magically* get better, but because each day spent afloat was more proof that I was capable of floating for another day.

I wasn't slacking or falling further behind: I was strategically half-assing parts of life because that's all I had the capacity for.

It didn't matter what I did or didn't do the day before. It didn't matter what I thought I'd be capable of tomorrow. Any action that wasn't "I give up" was enough.

I hope you can give yourself permission to redefine what "enough" is too. Instead of thinking of how far behind we are on our goals, do the bare minimum to stay above the surface.

If we can learn to do what it takes to not lose, we can ride out any storm for days, weeks, months, or even years.

Pause, Process, Persist

In an interview with *The A.V. Club* about their career-altering hit "Float On" (feel free to start singing), Modest Mouse singer Isaac Brock explained he just wanted to write something positive and uplifting for a change:

> It was a completely conscious thing. I was just kind of fed up with how bad sh** had been going, and how dark everything was, with bad news coming from everywhere . . . I just want to feel good for a day.

I think that's the perfect sentiment we can carry forward with us for the rest of this book.

If we start by not making things worse, we're *already better off.*

When our brains are screaming at us to go full YOLO ("you only live once") and eat Oreos by the sleeveful . . .

When the desire is to "do the same thing, but *harder,*" even when we know it doesn't work . . .

When we feel like we're falling further and further behind on everything . . .

We can pause and process what's really going on. We can take a breath. We can ask ourselves, "Is this working?" And then we can decide the next step.

And if the next right step is back toward where we started? Amazing.

We can have grace for our situation and compassion for the fact that life is hard. We can decide to half-ass or coast or quietly quit on parts of life right now. No matter what we've failed at before, or how far behind we think we are on our goals, treading water might be the most important thing we can do.

Now, we probably instinctively *know* what we can do to stay afloat and not lose.

Instead of lamenting how we haven't reached some arbitrary number on the scale, we can try to make every other meal a healthy one, and that's good enough for now.

Instead of getting upset that we're behind on our 5K training, we can just put on our running shoes and go for a quick walk-jog, which counts as a complete workout for today.

Instead of groaning that we're not crushing it at work, we can remind ourselves, "Wait a second, considering everything going on right now, I'm impressed I haven't fallen apart completely."

If we get good at treading water, we get to see what tomorrow brings.

And we can return to our tread-water strategy at any point in the future, no matter what happens. When another unexpected life event shows up, we don't have to come to a dead stop or make things worse. We just move into tread-water mode and confidently weather that storm too for as long as it takes.

It doesn't matter why we fell off the boat. There will be time for that later.

It doesn't matter what we didn't do yesterday, or what must get done tomorrow.

Let's narrow our focus to make sure we stay afloat today.

As long as we don't make things worse, as long as we keep our heads above water, as long as we don't lose, we get to see tomorrow.

Returning to Modest Mouse: "We'll all float on, okay?"

Key Insights

Don't make things worse. After any mistake, failure, or setback, we often make decisions that make future progress more challenging. We might waste precious energy by continuing to do the wrong thing without asking, "Is this working?" If we pause, it gives us a chance to stop moving down the wrong path. When compared with regression, staying where we are is a great alternative.

Expect less, do less. We don't need to swim faster. We don't need to keep trying to do all the things. We need to realize that we're struggling, and we're asking too much of ourselves. We can narrow our focus and expectations to what we're actually capable of right now. Resetting our expectations should feel good. Treading water should feel heroic. As long as we stay afloat, we get to see what tomorrow brings.

Stop trying to win. Don't lose. When we try to keep up with everything, particularly when life is crazy, we burn ourselves out. We can half-ass things when life calls for it, especially when the alternative is giving up. One healthy meal. One exercise. Reading one page. Any action that's different from "I quit" can be enough.

Pause, process, persist. So much of life happens in autopilot mode. When we pause and take a breath, it gives us the much needed mental space to slow down and find out if what we're doing is helping or hurting us. A pause is not moving backward. Compared with making things worse, a pause is the correct next step.

THE PACT FRAMEWORK

Pause

Accept

Change

Try

3

A IS FOR ACCEPT

Why "Normal" Isn't Normal, and That's Normal

You keep using that word. I do not think it means what you think it means.

—Inigo Montoya to the scoundrel Vizzini, *The Princess Bride*

Now that we've added "P for Pause" to our tool kit, things *should* get better, right? Maybe! But things also may get worse! Because life is absurd and so much of it is out of our control.

In order for us to take our next step, we need a new life skill. One that might change your life like it did mine.

Enter "acceptance."

As a recovering overachiever, I used to believe that acceptance was a sign of weakness. I thought it meant giving up all ambition, letting myself off the hook, and enabling lazy behavior. So I made things worse instead: I set high standards and remained unbelievably critical of myself, always felt behind, and never felt "enough." I know. Super fun!

Fortunately, I couldn't have been more wrong. Acceptance is the most important skill that helped me navigate these last few years.

Instead of lamenting about life not going a certain way, or complaining that things didn't work out the way I expected, acceptance taught me to see things for how they actually *are*.

Depending on when you read this, we might be in the middle of yet another once-in-a-lifetime, world-changing event that nobody saw coming. Personally, at the time of this writing, I could point to ten things that have me concerned.

I just paused to gesture wildly in every direction, so feel free to do the same.

The only truth is that we will never be able to accurately predict what life will throw at us next week, let alone next month or next year.

Which leaves us with two choices.

We can spend all day raging at the universe when things don't go the way they *should*, or we can get to work accepting things for how they are now. We can get mad at ourselves for not magically developing the skills to plan better, or we can learn to prepare for whatever life throws at us and say, "Okay, what's next?"

We'll start with the most common problem when it comes to acceptance, and then get into what to do about it.

The "Back to Normal" Fallacy: There Is No Normal

We have a normal morning routine. We have a normal workweek. We have a normal way of eating. We have a normal workout schedule.

When we think of "normal," what we really mean is "predictable." Knowable. Expected. Planned.

But then life happens.

Parents and caretakers know all too well that when a routine is thrown out the window, chaos reigns supreme. We feel like we're caught in a storm, getting tossed around, desperately waiting for things to get "back to normal."

A "normal" where we have some semblance of control over our lives again. Because not being in control is uncomfortable.

The problem, of course, is that our lives aren't completely our own. We have other complications like families or babies or jobs or dogs that "accidentally" ate the cat's poop and then barfed on the carpet in the middle of the night.

For many of us, "normal" isn't coming back any time soon. And we're not doing ourselves any favors by waiting for life to be any different than it is right now.

The longer we wait for "back to normal," the more we reinforce an "all-or-nothing" mindset. Worse, when we tell ourselves that we can only make progress when things are normal, we're training ourselves to give up as soon as things get busy again.

Right now, "busy" is our normal.

"Normal" is not synonymous with "predictable."

If 80 percent of our days are spent dealing with unpredictable schedules with kids or work that's chaotic, *that's* the actual normal part! The real unlocks start to happen once we embrace and accept the fact that right now, today, with all of its messiness, is normal. Speaking of, here's my favorite "normal" story.

* * *

I rediscovered golf during the pandemic and stumbled across a podcast called *Chasing Scratch*. Its hosts, Mike Shade and Eli Strait, are two college buddies in different states documenting their quest to become "scratch" golfers[5] while still being great dads, dedicated husbands, reliable employees, and so on. Reaching scratch is a feat fewer than 2 percent of golfers ever accomplish.

During one episode, Mike and Eli asked a few nutrition questions that I could help answer, so I emailed to offer guidance and support. A short conversation later, we paired the two with Nerd Fitness coach Matt Myers, who learned the ins and outs of their lives and built a strategy for their crazy schedules.

The success of their podcast is due to Mike and Eli's relatability, so it was no surprise when relatable challenges popped up.

Mike kept apologizing to Matt for life getting in the way: He needed to make an unexpected trip to his daughter's school, work would get busy, a meeting would run long, or a side project would require unexpected overtime.

Often, Mike would say the thing that we all find ourselves saying: "But next week things should get back to normal." A normal, predictable future that Mike fully believed was just around the corner.

The problem, of course, was that the next week something else

---

5 Overly simplified, this means having an average score of even par on an average golf course.

would pop up, and the apology train would start once again. After a month or so of these apologies, Matt sent an honest voice message to Mike that shook his world: "I worry you think there's a 'normal' you're going to get back to. That 'normal' doesn't exist anymore."

Mike's "normal" was anything but normal!

The podcast began as a fun side hobby to stay connected with his best friend, and it accidentally became a huge success and had become Mike's full-time job. His new normal involved running a small business, working from home instead of in an office, with new responsibilities and a new schedule, while also still handling the rest of his life responsibilities.

His life was completely different from what it had been a year before.

After this realization, Mike stopped apologizing for life happening and started accepting reality. Rather than beating himself up for not being perfect or delaying progress until some magical future when life went "back to normal," he and Matt built a flexible strategy that could change when life changed.

Mike embraced the mantra "There is no normal!"[6]

Mike had a menu of different workouts of different lengths that could be swapped out at the last second depending on the day. He had backup options for healthy meals when his daughter's after-school activities ran late. He identified parts of the day when his schedule was less volatile, which gave him a better

---

6 Through a series of fortunate events, Mike and Eli got to interview actor Carl Weathers just days before he passed away, who shared his own motivational mantra of "there is no tomorrow."

opportunity to do the most important goal before the day inevitably went off the rails.

Rather than planning for perfection, Mike learned to make imperfect progress with an imperfect schedule.

Meanwhile, cohost Eli was navigating a hectic schedule himself: In addition to his regular day job, his podcasting responsibilities, and his home responsibilities, he coached his two sons' traveling basketball teams and had recently become the local high school coach as well. And then things took a left turn. After months of pain, Eli had hip surgery, missing the entire 2024 golf year. You might wonder, "How does a golf podcast survive when half of the podcasting team can't play golf?" With transparency, acceptance, and a few dozen inside jokes.

For us fans, it was encouraging to hear Mike and Eli navigate their setbacks with grace and humor. We listen *because of these challenges*, not in spite of them.

How can we carry similar attitudes into our own lives?

We can accept that life will never be as predictable as we'd like.

We can stop getting frustrated when our schedule falls apart and start expecting it. We can prepare for our plan to not go according to plan. And finally, we can accept reality.

The "back to normal" fallacy assumes there is a magical, predictable "normal" life hiding just around the corner. The sooner we accept that our current "normal" is normal, the sooner we can choose to act differently:

- Having backup workout plans to switch to when life gets in the way.

- Freezing backup meals to heat up when we're just too damn tired to cook.
- Identifying one or two "tread water" activities to fall back on during crazy days: a short walk, a guided meditation, a five-minute workout.

When we're no longer surprised when our day goes to hell, that's when things start to get interesting.

Instead of wishing things were different, we start to see life as it really is.

We stop trying to build a better plan. We accept reality and prepare for more chaos.

Let Go, Quit, Give Up! Acceptance Isn't Lazy; It's Smart

I've spent a most of my adult life trying to do it all, be it all, have it all.

Every day, I would wake up and immediately think of all the tasks and goals and things that needed to get done so that I could be "caught up." I also had my list of life goals that I was behind on too: I want to write more books and read all the classics and see more movies and get better at multiple musical instruments and travel more and volunteer more and be in better shape and become a better golfer. Oh, and I want to spend more time with friends and family, prioritize my mental health, get enough sleep, and so on.

For years I told myself I was one lifehack away from being able to do it all. After optimizing my work schedule, I started to optimize my free time too. Everything had to be done efficiently so that I could get to the next thing, which also had to be optimized so that I could get to the next thing, and so on. Unfortunately, the only result of this was trapping myself in a prison of expectation. I woke up every morning already feeling behind.

(Yeah, I'm exhausted just typing this out.)

I used to think this gave me the best chance to get it all done and stop feeling behind. I had a steadfast belief that I *could* do it all if I just wanted it enough, planned well enough, and put the right plan in place.

I thought I was being ambitious.

I was actually just falling into what author Oliver Burkeman calls the "efficiency trap." The more efficient I became, the more things ended up on my plate that needed to be efficiently dealt with.

I was trying to win a game that couldn't be won.

As long as I could pretend that I was just *one* productivity hack away from being able to get everything done, then I never had to make tough choices about what to prioritize. I didn't want to admit it, but I was living in a fantasyland where I could magically find the time to do everything and reach all my goals and still have time to relax. I was chasing an impossible dream.

As Burkeman further explains in his book *Four Thousand Weeks*, life is simply too rich to experience it all:

> The more wonderful experiences you succeed in having, the more additional wonderful experiences you start to

feel you could have, or ought to have, on top of the ones you've already had, with the result that the feeling of existential overwhelm gets worse.

At first, this made me frustrated. Then I realized I was practicing what he calls life procrastination. I kept trying to do everything because that was less scary than accepting the limitations of being mortal with a limited time frame.

The fact that we cannot do it all and will never be "caught up" is the only thing that gives life meaning.

If we could actually do *everything* and then be *done*, nothing would really matter, because we could always do everything eventually.

Here in reality, we have to make choices. Some options are closed off. Saying yes to anything means saying no to countless other things. This is where we need acceptance.

Once we stop needing to "get ahead" or be "caught up" to feel okay, we realize we're already okay.

In writer Dyske Suematsu's essay "The Art of Giving Up," he tells the story of a friend playing the guitar at a Christmas party. This friend used to be a professional musician, but now works as an architect. Suematsu expressed sadness that his friend was no longer pursuing music as a career.

The friend's reply surprised him: "Life is a process of giving up."

As he explained: "'Giving up,' in this sense, isn't the same as quitting. [My] friend was still playing guitar; he just wasn't pursuing it professionally." Like many folks going after a creative or athletic career in a competitive field, "giving up" professionally often doesn't mean it's the end of that activity.

Instead, it's giving up the pressure that comes from trying to make it work as a career. Suematsu continues, "Contrary to what one might assume from the connotations of the expression 'giving up,' this is done in order to enjoy life more."

It can be liberating to say, "I'm letting this go."

Instead of making minimal progress on a lot of things, always feeling behind, we can close a few doors, and enjoy our time with the few things that actually matter.

I shared this sentiment in my newsletter, and reader Marie replied with some delightfully transparent and accepting wisdom:

> My mantra became "It's okay to say no to good things," since there will always be more good things than I have time to do.

Life is making choices, and that includes setting down some expectations. It means giving up on some goals (for now, at least). It means making peace with the fact that we will never get "caught up," because there will always be more things that can be done.

It also means saying no to more things without guilt.

And not just saying no to the stuff we don't want to do, but also saying no to many things we *do* want to do but don't have the bandwidth for right now!

By learning to let go, we just might find some time to do the few things that matter right now:

- Maybe it's okay that we give up on running a marathon for now, because we're more interested in trying fitness classes with our new partner. Great.
- Maybe it's okay to set aside our dream of writing a novel while we're raising young kids. This doesn't need to be something else we feel behind on.
- Maybe it's okay to let go of the pressure we feel to over-achieve at work and be a supermom and volunteer at the school while also being impossibly fit.

Letting go and giving up isn't letting ourselves off the hook or abandoning our ambition. It's finally removing the pressure we feel each day that we're already behind. It's accepting that we cannot do it all and that's okay.

Avoidance Is Intoxicating; Acceptance Is Courageous

I've never felt more personally attacked or understood than after reading the following quote from the seventeenth-century philosopher Blaise Pascal:

> All of humanity's problems stem from man's inability to sit quietly in a room alone.

Most of us (myself *definitely* included) have some aspect of life that just isn't working the way we want it to right now. The part that makes us uncomfortable when we think about it. The reason *behind* the reason we feel like we're struggling. The thought that wakes us up at 4 a.m. to remind us it's not going anywhere.

- A conversation that *needs* to happen related to our job, our family, or our relationship.
- A potential health problem that's scary (while we come up with more excuses to avoid calling the doctor).
- An event from our past that we never properly dealt with (or sought therapy for).

No matter what it is, it makes us uncomfortable, and our brains do *not* like feeling this way. Which is why it tells us, "Let's not deal with that yet. Don't open Pandora's box[7]. Who knows what else might pop out! Keep that lid closed and cram that thought down and hide it in the corner!"

For those of us who avoid our uncomfortable thoughts, we deal with them in one of two unhealthy ways:

- **Avoidance Method #1: Kick the can down the road.** We pick a future date or a milestone and say we'll "deal with it then." After this work project. After the kids go to college. After things slow down.

  Interestingly, when we reach that milestone, our

7 In Greek myth, Pandora was a woman whose curiosity led her to open a sealed container that unleashed curses upon mankind. The phrase "opening Pandora's box" has evolved to mean "this will have unintended consequences."

brains come up with yet another reason to kick the can *just* a bit farther. We say Future Us can deal with it.

- **Avoidance Method #2: Drown it out.** The *second* we're anxious, bored, or uncomfortable, we reach for the digital pacifier in our pocket, our smartphone. We can open social media and watch a video of a three-legged dog named Champion getting adopted from the shelter. We can doomscroll the news, or put on a podcast to let *other* people's thoughts drown out our own. As long as we numb ourselves until the scary thought goes away, mission accomplished.

Our ego *thinks* it's doing us a favor by protecting us from the uncomfortable stuff we're avoiding. Unfortunately, this creates the exact opposite result.

First, avoidance can make the problem *actually* worse, which will make us want to avoid it even more. Like *not* going to the dentist when we have a cavity, or ignoring the "overdue loan" notice in the mail. Every day we wait, the problem gets bigger.

But you already knew that.

Second, here's another fun fact of avoidance: Despite what we want to believe, we're not *nearly* as clever at hiding our uncomfortable thoughts as we think. They're influencing our lives whether or not we realize it.

On an episode of *The Tim Ferriss Show*, author Brené Brown was asked about our tendency to avoid issues *we know* are hiding underneath the surface. Host Tim Ferriss asked how to help people who were "afraid to open Pandora's box" and wanted to wait to process uncomfortable thoughts until later.

Her response caught me off guard:

> Are you under the impression that you're living outside of the box or in the box? . . . Because you're living inside Pandora's box.

The thoughts and problems we're avoiding aren't locked up safely. They're impacting *every* conversation, decision, action, and experience we have every day. They're why we resort to unhealthy coping mechanisms or emotional outbursts directed at the wrong thing: taking out our anger on people who don't deserve it, using substances to numb or avoid or forget, or procrastinating in weird ways. All the while pretending like things are *just great, thanks for asking.*

This is when we have to ask ourselves some tough questions. Maybe yelling at our kids for the LEGO pieces on the floor isn't *really* about the LEGO pieces on the floor, but the fact that we hate our job. Maybe we're not actually mad at the person who made that left turn, but the fact that life at home is really dysfunctional right now.

I have good news and bad news. As Buddhist nun and author Pema Chödrön points out in *When Things Fall Apart*:

> We regard discomfort in any form as bad news . . .
> Instead of being bad news, these are actually very clear moments that teach us where it is that we're holding back.

Life is desperately trying to show us where we are blocked and where we need to shine a light. The sooner we open the box, the sooner we can start to deal with whatever is in there.

If we're lucky, the problems we've been avoiding are manageable and can be dealt with swiftly: The unpaid credit card bill wasn't as high as we thought. The irregular mole on our back was benign. Our spouse or boss appreciated our vulnerability.

But sometimes, those problems are worse than expected. Which is also good, because we're finally doing something about it. If the credit card bill is *massive,* it's not going to get any smaller than it is right now. If the mole *is* skin cancer, detection *today* is better than tomorrow. If the relationship or job explodes, the sooner we can make amends or move on.

Speaking as somebody with expert-level avoidance skills, I've worked hard to lean in to uncomfortable thoughts and ask what I can learn from them. And every time, there's one emotion that comes to the surface after I finally face a fear, make a decision, or work on the thing I've been avoiding: relief.

Dealing with what comes after can be difficult, but it's far less painful than living a life of avoidance for months or years or decades. Acceptance asks us to see life for what it is and not shy away from the tough parts:

- We need to tell our spouse that we're drowning trying to manage the house and kids and our job and we need help.
- We need to accept that we need help for a disorder or addiction.

- We need to admit to ourselves that we're on the wrong career path and it's time for a change.

All of this requires growth and courage: sitting alone with our thoughts, asking for help, leaning in to discomfort, and sharing our truth openly. When we open the box and shine a light inside, only then can we get to work dealing with what's in there.

Acceptance Means "Yes, and . . ."

This entire chapter is built around contradictions.

We have to embrace that "normal" isn't normal. We have to give up more often to get more out of life. We have to find ways to get comfortable with the uncomfortable lessons life is trying to teach us.

It's paradoxes all the way down.

There's some powerful psychology at work here.

It's called Dialectical Behavior Therapy (DBT), which I realize is three fancy words in a trench coat, so let's just focus on the first word for now.

"Dialectical" is best explained by author F. Scott Fitzgerald, who says in his essay "The Crack-Up":

> The test of a first-rate intelligence is the ability to hold two opposed ideas in the mind at the same time, and still retain the ability to function.

You are currently reading this book, which means you *definitely* have first-rate intelligence. Also, you look nice today, and I love what you've done with your hair.

Back to DBT.

This therapy was developed in the early 1980s by Marsha Linehan, PhD, to help patients with borderline personality disorder or patients who have suicidal thoughts. It was thirty years later when Dr. Linehan finally shared why she had dedicated her life to developing this groundbreaking therapy: She had been a suicidal teenager who spent two years in an institution, eventually crawling her way out of the darkness and becoming a psychologist and therapist to help others.

Since its development, DBT has helped not only those with the above conditions but countless others who are simply trying to navigate life in modern society. It's a type of therapy that can help those with perfectionist tendencies, or those who feel that they must be in control of every outcome in order to find peace.

Not that any of us could *possibly* relate, of course.

DBT can be helpful because it helps us embrace acceptance and the complexity of life. Here's the next line of that Fitzgerald quote:

> One should, for example, be able to see that things are hopeless yet be determined to make them otherwise.

I bet you can relate to the feeling he's conveying here. Parts of life might feel overwhelming right now, but that doesn't mean there's nothing to be done. It means we can practice acceptance of our crappy situation and then say "and here's what I can do today."

Interestingly, this ability to accept and take action doesn't just apply to DBT.

It's also the foundational rule of improvisational comedy, or "improv."

During an improv scene, somebody will suggest an absurd scene or situation, and the best responses will then build on it with the philosophy of "Yes, and . . ."

If somebody declares they're a circus bear on a unicycle, their scene partner might build on this by saying, "Yes, and I am a polar bear mechanic who repairs unicycles." If another person says they discovered the moon is made of cheese, then their scene partner might say, "Yes, and I'm a lactose-intolerant astronaut mouse."

"Yes" implies that we accept the situation with absolute sincerity.

"And . . ." means that we build upon this with our actions.

What a delightful strategy for navigating the absurd paradoxes of life: compassionate honesty and acceptance of what's really happening.

If work sucks and we're navigating a chronic illness, we can say, "Yes, this is unfair. And I'm going to give myself some grace and finally ask for help."

If we know our kids are on summer vacation for the next month, we can say, "Yep, this is going to be crazy. I'm going to take on less responsibility at work and prioritize hikes with my daughters instead of going to the gym."

If we are despondent about the state of the world, we can say, "Yep, there's a lot wrong right now AND I'm going to vote in my local elections and support charities that are important to me."

Acceptance is the only way we can function in a world that feels contradictory, because it lets us embrace those contradictions.

Despite the hectic nature of our days, we still can take steps in our own lives to prove to ourselves that all hope isn't lost.

YES, life is challenging and we have some real limitations.

AND here's what we're planning to focus our efforts on today.

Key Insights

Beware the "back to normal" fallacy. "Normal" and "predictable" aren't interchangeable. Once we stop pretending that we'll get back to yesterday's normal and start embracing today's chaos, we can start to see reality more clearly. When we prepare for an unpredictable day, we stop chasing the perfect plan and allow ourselves to make imperfect progress.

Let go, give up, and quit. Acceptance isn't lazy, it's smart. When we keep pretending that we can get everything done with the right plan or schedule, it keeps us from making important decisions about how we should spend our limited time. We need to let go of trying to "catch up" on everything and let go of some goals or dreams that no longer fit. Only then we can get to work on the few things that matter.

Avoidance is alluring. Acceptance is courageous. It's easy to avoid the uncomfortable lessons life is trying to teach us. If we can find the courage to open Pandora's box and shine a light in there, we can see clearly just how big the problem we've been avoiding really is. Discomfort can be an amazing teacher if we sit with it. And when we accept the scary thought? We feel relief, because we're finally addressing the problem.

Acceptance means saying, "Yes, and . . ." Dialectical Behavioral Therapy helps us develop the skill of sitting with two opposing thoughts at the same time. The best way to do this is to act like an improv comic: "Yes, and . . ." Life is never black or white, nor all good or bad. Life is complex, and so are we. We can embrace this: "Yes, this is my unfair situation. And here's what is still within my control today."

THE PACT FRAMEWORK

Pause

Accept

Change

Try

4

C IS FOR CHANGE

What's Different This Time?

One Sunday morning the warm sun came up and—pop!—out of the egg came a tiny and very hungry caterpillar.

—*The Very Hungry Caterpillar* by Eric Carle

We're halfway through the PACT; we've done the Pause and Accept parts, so let's take the next step and talk about change. Specifically, why change is so damn hard and messy.

And we'll learn this lesson from an insect.

Do you know what *actually* happens when a caterpillar transforms into a butterfly?

If you're like me, you read Eric Carle's *The Very Hungry Caterpillar* as a kid. You flipped through the colorful pages about the cute little caterpillar eating through one apple, two pears, three plums, four strawberries, and five oranges. And then you read about how the caterpillar built "a small house, called a cocoon, around himself. He stayed inside for more than two weeks. Then he nibbled a hole in the cocoon, pushed his way out, and he was a beautiful butterfly!"

As kids, we assume it's a two-week cozy vacation where the caterpillar knits itself a cute little pair of colorful wings, and BAM! It emerges as a beautiful butterfly.

That's not actually how it happens.

It's less lovely and more Lovecraftian.

When a caterpillar goes into a chrysalis[8] to begin its transformation, *it literally eats itself*, releasing enzymes that dissolve the remainder of its body. A few specific cells are preserved while the rest becomes caterpillar soup.

Open a chrysalis at the wrong time, and caterpillar goo will pour out. I know. Nightmare fuel.

But truthfully, this caterpillar soup stage is the most critical step. While in the chrysalis, the caterpillar's remaining cells use the protein-rich goo to create a whole new body, wings, antennae, eyes, and legs. Only after it's gone through this disgusting transformation does it finally become the beautiful butterfly we all know and *most* of us love. (Personally, butterflies give me the heebie-jeebies.)

A butterfly's metamorphosis is a stunning accomplishment, like a can of alphabet soup organizing itself into *War and Peace*.

It's also the perfect metaphor for why change is so difficult, gross, and uncomfortable.

We're no longer who we *were,* and not yet who we want to *be.*

Change requires us to move through the in-between stage. Our caterpillar soup.

---

8 With apologies to Mr. Carle, butterflies come from chrysalises, while moths come from cocoons.

Fortunately, we just learned to accept reality, which means we can now start to think about change with a different mindset.

We need to first solve why we struggled with a particular change in the past, and then commit to doing things differently in the future.

We'll accomplish this by embracing two unlikely professions.

Solve the Mystery of Past Us with Curiosity, Not Judgment

As a kid who grew up before social media and cell phones, I can remember many rainy days gathered around the kitchen table playing Clue, a board game invented by Anthony E. Pratt in the 1940s.

For the uninitiated, this game involves a number of players in a mansion, trying to solve a murder. If you've ever been to a murder mystery dinner party, or read *Sherlock Holmes* or any Agatha Christie novel, this is exactly that, in board game form. Players must gather clues from the scene of the crime and explore various rooms in the mansion. Then they make an educated guess as to which character committed the crime and which weapon was used to do the deed:

- Was it Colonel Mustard with the candlestick in the billiard room?
- Maybe it was Professor Plum with the wrench in the library!
- It could possibly have been Mrs. Peacock with the revolver in the kitchen.

Now, my love of solving crimes wasn't limited to just board games. When I wasn't playing Clue, I was reading my favorite book series that involved less murder but just as much mystery: Encyclopedia Brown. These books revolved around a grade-school boy named "Encyclopedia" who ran a detective agency out of his garage for twelve cents a case. He also helped his father (the police chief of Idaville) solve more challenging cases over dinner.[9]

Why was I so obsessed with Clue and this child detective? Simple. They made detective work *fun*. Even the murders.

When a detective shows up at a crime scene, they have a specific sequence of things they do. Maybe they find some evidence or uncover fingerprints that need to be analyzed. They might speak with witnesses and start to do a deep dive into the victim's background.

Eventually they're identifying suspects, looking for motives, and narrowing down what happened. Hopefully, all this evidence leads to a Clue-like solution: "It was [X person], for [Y reasons] on [Z date]." Case closed!

Now, I probably didn't need to explain how crime scenes work, because you listen to the *My Favorite Murder* podcast to wind down, or watch *Law & Order: SVU* or *Only Murders in the Building*. I'm now realizing that we Americans have a slight addiction to murder and true-crime stories. Shockingly, we also struggle with sleep and anxiety. Couldn't possibly be related.

Anyway, on to the fun stuff.

---

9 Real Talk: Police Chief Brown should probably be fired for sharing open investigations with a ten-year-old, but those books are still very fun.

We are going to conduct a completely nonjudgmental crime scene investigation of Past Us. Feel free to give yourself a fun detective name like Hercule Poirot or Nancy Drew, and a mysterious backstory. A fun hat, corncob pipe, and giant magnifying glass are optional but encouraged.

Next, imagine there is a chalk outline of your past "attempt to change" on the ground.

Don't worry, that was Past Us, a completely different person from who we are now. As the quote widely attributed to writer Alan Watts goes, "You're under no obligation to be the same person you were five minutes ago."

In some scenes, it was a personal challenge we struggled with and our demise was self-inflicted. In other situations, it might have been a freak accident outside of our control. Sometimes we'll discover we tried to do too much, while in other scenarios we'll discover we didn't change enough.

Let's imagine we're playing Clue.

Except, instead of Colonel Mustard and a candlestick in the library, it's probably something more like:

- "Fascinating! Work sucked, I was overwhelmed, and I blew off my afternoon run!"
- "Interesting! I got busy and my brain immediately reverted to all-or-nothing thinking and I gave up the second I couldn't be perfect."
- "A clue! I ate a whole pint of ice cream this afternoon. My kids were screaming, my mom called with a health scare, and I skipped therapy this week!"

Elementary, my dear friend.

No matter the cause, understanding why and how Past Us struggled will help us develop the self-awareness required for true change and progress in the future.

A quick word of advice:

When analyzing why we failed in the past, what looks like a "motivation" problem is often a "resources" problem in disguise.

We had too much on our plate. We were carrying too much of the "invisible load" at home and with the kids. We have taken on too much responsibility at work. *AND* we tried to build a completely new habit that required more time on top of that. No wonder we burned ourselves out!

As we're investigating the mystery of Past Us, we can stop chastising ourselves for not being motivated enough and dive deeper into what's really going on under the surface.

It requires us to look into our past with a different framework from the one we normally bring with us. And we can learn this lesson from the world's most enthusiastic soccer (football) coach.

For many, *Ted Lasso* was a sitcom that provided much-needed hope and escape during the COVID-19 pandemic. In one episode, the titular Ted mentions a quote from the poet Walt Whitman, **"Be curious, not judgmental."**

Lasso mentions how helpful this sentiment has been throughout his life, and how it allows him to outsmart judgmental adversaries who underestimate him. Now, apparently Whitman never actually wrote these words,[10] but I don't want to live in a world in which Ted Lasso is incorrect. So, let's assume Whitman stated this and then went on to write "O Captain! My Captain!" It'll be our secret because nonjudgmental curiosity is a great sentiment to bring along for the ride.

We can be curious as to why we responded in a certain way.

We can be curious about the series of events that led to the untimely demise of Past Us.

We can be curious about why our brain decided to interpret certain situations one way or another.

Of course, there's a *big* difference between knowing what needs to be changed and being able to change it, but nonjudgmental curiosity is an amazing step that can break past cycles.

We can then take this information and apply it to the next goal or challenge we embark upon. No matter what we failed at, there's a bigger lesson we can take from it.

Each failed attempt to change is a lesson taught by Past Us. It tells the truth as plainly as possible, if we can find the courage to examine the crime scene closely. If we ask questions and go a bit deeper, we can reflect on *why* we failed at these things.

Let's walk through an example tracing the clues back to the source.

---

10 According to Snopes.com, the words appeared in a 1986 advice column by Marguerite and Marshall Shearer, but it's anyone's guess whether that was its first usage.

Last week, we skipped our workout. Sure, we can say we were busy, but let's dig deeper and ask "why" a few times.

How many times should we ask? Five.

According to Taiichi Ohno, the father of the Toyota Production System,[11] asking "why?" five times is usually enough to find the root of a problem and get to work on a solution.

It's okay that we're not Toyota Corollas on an assembly line. The "Five Whys" method still works for us curious detectives.

Let's try it out!

I am frustrated with myself. Why?

Because I skipped my workout this morning. Why?

Because I slept through my alarm. Why?

Because I didn't get to bed until midnight. Why?

Because I couldn't stop doomscrolling on my phone. Why?

Because I'm burned out from work and taking care of the kids, and scrolling on my phone at the end of the night is the only time I have for myself!

Whoa.

Suddenly "I missed my workout and I'm lazy" has become a realization that we're not getting the support we need, and we've resorted to unhealthy coping mechanisms (like mindlessly scrolling social media) to disassociate and numb our brains at the end of the day.

Maybe we can talk with our partner about what's really going on at work, or ask the kids to chip in with laundry and cooking.

---

11 Hat tip to Mike Sowden of the Everything Is Amazing newsletter for sharing this tip with me!

If we keep asking why, each question gets us a bit closer to understanding past struggles and what we can choose to do differently.

Sometimes, asking why can reveal an uncomfortable truth that nudges us to finally address it. Here's a *completely hypothetical example* that I made up off the top of my head:

I can't write my book; I have to rearrange my bookshelf. Why?

Because I don't *really* want to work on my book now. Why?

Because my insecurity around submitting something less than perfect scares me. Why?

Because I have imposter syndrome and I'm worried my book's not good enough. Why?

Because I don't feel like I'm "enough" and I care too much about the outcome. Why?

Because I'm human. I need to realize that "perfectionism" is a fallacy. I need to let go of expectations and just do the work.

Whoa.

Rearranging my bookshelf was actually downstream of the uncomfortable fact that I am overly focused on outcomes and unattainable perfection, and it's paralyzing.

Eventually, I allowed myself to let go of needing a certain outcome. I gave myself permission to write an imperfect book.

Again, this was a totally hypothetical example.

Don't Set Goals; Conduct Experiments Like a Scientist

When I was little, I would wake up at 6 a.m. every weekday to watch *Mr. Wizard's World* on the Nickelodeon channel. Years later, I moved on to *Bill Nye the Science Guy* and *Beakman's World* (though I'm still not sure why there was an anthropomorphic rat named Lester who hung out with Beakman).

Why did I watch these shows?

Because they made science *fun*!

Mr. Wizard would invite a "neighborhood kid" over to his "house" (I didn't realize they were paid actors on a studio set, but I was seven). The experiments were conducted with a lovely, joyful curiosity.

Mr. Wizard and the kids were scientists trying to find out what would happen. Okay, it was mostly Mr. Wizard playing pranks on helpless children through these experiments. There were a lot of explosions and chemicals and unexpected surprises that made my little brain vibrate with curiosity: *I wonder what's going to happen?!*

We're going to become scientists too. Please remove your detective hat and Inverness cape, and please put on your lab coat. Feel free to imagine you're a famous scientist like Nikola Tesla or Marie Curie.

Speaking of, can I take a quick detour to talk about just how much of a trailblazer Marie Curie was? Well, it's my book, so I'm just going to do it.

You might know Curie shared the 1903 Nobel Prize in Physics for discovering radioactivity.[12] She won another Nobel Prize in 1911 in Chemistry, and remains the only person in history to win the award in two different scientific fields.

---

12 Frustratingly, the Nobel committee had planned on giving the award only to Henri Becquerel (for discovering radiation) and Marie's husband, Pierre Curie. When Pierre complained and campaigned for his wife, Marie was finally recognized as well.

But did you also know that after winning two Nobel Prizes, she invented the mobile X-ray unit that helped win World War I?

(Feel free to audibly gasp and cover your mouth for effect.)

Curie hypothesized that the sooner a wounded soldier was diagnosed, the sooner and more accurately they could be treated. The result? Fewer infections, fewer unnecessary amputations, and more confident treatment by field surgeons and nurses. Over one million soldiers were x-rayed, untold numbers of lives were saved, and the mobile X-ray unit fundamentally changed mobile medical treatment forever.

Did I share all this because Marie Curie was a badass? Absolutely.

Is she also going to help us make more informed decisions moving forward? Of course.

We can skip the "handle radioactive material" part, and just focus on the "scientific method" part.

We've already done the first step: Observe the world and come up with a question we want answered. We played detective and observed our past, so we should have some ideas on what we want to do differently the next time.

Next, we form a hypothesis. This is an educated guess at what we think might help us build our next habit or improve our routine:

- "Going to the gym with my friend in the morning will make me more likely to enjoy it than going alone at night."
- "Joining a writing club will make me more likely to follow through on my fan fiction than writing at home alone."

- "Setting up my dating profile with more candid photos of me and my dog would be better than more selfies of me in my car."

The experiment is something we're willing to try, informed by past experiments and our detective work. We are guessing what we *think* could happen, and then we get to try it out and see what actually happens.

Here's the key difference between a nebulous goal and an experiment: a time frame! Experiments have end dates so that the results can be analyzed.

We're not asking "How soon can I accomplish this goal?" but rather "When can I evaluate to see if this experiment is working *for me?*"

By picking a time frame (for example, thirty days), we get to gather data, record our results, and decide whether or not to continue the experiment. It's long enough to see a trend, but not so long that we get distracted, bored, or run out of energy to finish the experiment.

At the end of that time frame, it gives us a chance to pause, accept the results, and then decide to change or keep going (hey, that's a PACT!).

At Nerd Fitness, we call this the "Zoom In, Zoom Out" method. We pick our experiment and a time frame, then focus on the experiment we're conducting:

"I'm going to fill out one page of my journal each morning for a month and see if that helps me find some clarity about what's next for my career."

"We're going to have a family game night each Wednesday over the summer to see if this is something my kids and I can get excited about that doesn't involve screens."

"For the next month I'm going to cook three meals at home each week instead of eating fast food for every meal, and see if it is sustainable."

Then, at a predetermined date, we can zoom out and look at how the month went. Sometimes, we discover that we didn't enjoy the experiment, or the results weren't what we expected. Sometimes, we are happy with the results, and we decide to continue the experiment for another month without making any adjustments. Either one is great, and neither requires judgment or criticism. We're scientists conducting an experiment.

I remember one of my favorite success stories from Nerd Fitness, involving a courageous client with a willingness to experiment. She came to us frustrated with a lack of progress despite dieting for years. She was miserable, exhausted, and frustrated.

Fortunately, she trusted her coach Evan Jones enough to try an experiment: She was going to eat *more* food (specifically protein) for exactly one month. She would track the scale, take photos and measurements, and keep track of how she *felt*.

This experimental mindset gave her permission to make this change, particularly scary for somebody who had been bombarded with toxic diet culture for most of her life. Interestingly, by eating more, she had more energy and felt less lethargic, which allowed her to enjoy herself at the gym, and she discovered a love for strength training.

Her mindset around nutrition shifted from "I'm depriving

myself of joy to fit into these pants" to "I'm fueling my workouts and building strength." That one month turned into ongoing, sustainable progress without frustration.

Experiments allow us to try differently, without judgment or feeling overwhelmed. We're just trying something out for a few weeks. We can hyper-focus on the experiment, and then occasionally zoom out and decide if we want to keep going or not.

No matter the outcome, the experiment is a success if we learn something.

How to Pick the Right Variable for Your Experiment

If there's one part of experimentation that people struggle with the most, it's picking the right variable to test. It's easy to get caught up in trying to do the most optimized workout or follow "the best diet" for the fastest results. We're bombarded with ways to become more efficient daily. Which isn't surprising: There is a *lot* of money to be made in hustle culture and "human optimization."

Think of the pedometers and sleep-tracking rings and smart beds and smart watches tracking every movement. Or social media overrun with "alpha warriors" sharing their protocols and strategies and hacks and tactics. This whole industry is built on the idea that if some information is good, then *more* information is better. If some optimization is good, then the *MOST* optimization is best.

Yes, sometimes having more data can be helpful!

But other times, having more data, or tracking the wrong data, can actually make us focus on the wrong stat, ask the wrong question, or make things worse.

My friend and speech coach Mike Pacchione joked he had to stop wearing an AppleWatch because he felt like he was disappointing Apple CEO Tim Cook every time he didn't get enough sleep or exercise.

Personally, I had to stop wearing my fitness tracking devices too because they caused me to focus on the wrong thing. I would wake up in the middle of the night and my brain would say, "This is ruining my 'sleep score,'" which would make it even harder for me to fall back asleep. I started to get so concerned about step counts and closing "exercise rings" and hitting "sleep scores" that I developed anxiety around being less than optimized. I realized that was too much data for me.

By the way, "know thyself" doesn't just apply to exercise data, but to our diets as well.

Some dietary strategies like "track every macronutrient" or "count every calorie" or "weigh every ingredient" can be informative and helpful for some, but can lead others to develop a fear around breaking rigid food rules and not being perfect or "eating clean."

As we're deciding which experiments are worth conducting, we can look at past experiences to decide which metrics are helpful for our brains, and which data points are harmful. This should allow us to hopefully make more informed decisions on what our next experiment will measure.

Here's my favorite dystopian story from corporate America that shows data tracking gone wrong.

As Bloomberg's Matt Levine reported, in 2024, Wells Fargo fired a bunch of their remote employees for cheating at work. These employees were "simulating keyboard activity" with a program/device that automatically typed keys or jiggled their mouse when they weren't actually at their computer. It seems like a silly thing to install, until you learn more about *why* they installed it.

They were being remotely tracked by their bosses to see how many hours they were active on their computers. So the employees gave them exactly that: active hours. I'm sure many of them also did their jobs well and satisfied all of their responsibilities, but they were being monitored for computer activity, which led to a bizarre solution.

As the investor Charlie Munger once said, "Show me the incentive and I'll show you the outcome." The path to a bad outcome is often paved with bad metrics! This doesn't just apply to remote employees gaming the system, but also the metrics we can choose to track for our personal experiments.

Let's run through a few examples:

You're reading this book, so I assume you're a fellow bookworm.

Many people love to set goals like "read fifty books this year." I get it! I really do. But this incentive can encourage the wrong outcome. It nudges us to read shorter books instead of tackling larger classics we've always wanted to try. It might encourage us to speed-read instead of deeply understanding a challenging topic, or to stick with a bad book long after we've grown bored. All because we decided that "finishing more books" was the goal.

What if we picked a different metric to track? Instead of a yearlong goal, what if we experimented with "reading fifteen minutes each day?" In Leo Tolstoy's *War and Peace*, Prince Andrei is reflecting on how to handle a long, arduous journey, and shares the following pearl of wisdom with his friend Pierre:

> A man on a thousand mile walk has to forget his goal and say to himself every morning, "Today I'm going to cover twenty-five miles and then rest up and sleep."

Pretty good advice for getting anywhere or doing anything: Don't freak yourself out with how far you have to go. Do some of it today, and then do that again tomorrow. Comically, this is how I finally read *War and Peace*: a daily goal of reading at least one page.[13]

We can apply this to many other goals people love to set:

- "I'm going to bike 1,000 miles this year!"
- "I'm going to do 150 workouts this year!"
- "I'm going to lose 100 pounds this year!"
- "I'm going to finish more books this year!"

When we pick metrics like this, we're setting ourselves up for a midyear setback when life gets in the way:

---

13 Why yes, I did include a quote from *War and Peace* to wedge this humblebrag into the book.

January goes well (it always does), but then we get the flu in February and our kid gets sick in March. Suddenly we're so far behind pace that we get demoralized and give up on the big goal, even though it's only April!

We would have been better off setting a weekly or monthly goal, tracking a different metric, and having a way to try again whenever life happens:

- "I'm going to bike twenty-five miles each week."
- "I'm going to celebrate every time I do ten workouts."
- "I'm going to cook ten healthy meals each month."

We get to pick our experiments, and we get to pick the metric we're tracking. When we pick experiments and milestones and things that set us up to succeed, it gives us the best chance to make progress, even when life gets in the way.

Let the Great Experiment Begin!

There's a joke from comedian Jim Gaffigan, who explains his frustration when he sees really fit people in the gym: "What are you doing here? You're done!" Unfortunately, we know that's not how change works.

Whether we're trying to build a new routine, learn to meditate, or heal our relationship with food, we never get to be "done."

Temporary changes create temporary results, which means we need to rethink our relationship with change.

Like a caterpillar turning into a butterfly, transforming ourselves is complex and challenging and sometimes gross.

We can start by taking a few minutes to solve the mystery of Past Us. Like detectives, we can analyze clues and ask questions to dig to the root of the problem. We know most "motivation" problems are probably "resources" problems. Most important, we do all of this with curiosity, not judgment. We're gathering all the material we need to see how we can try again differently next time.

We can then look at the next thirty days like a fun experiment. We can put on our lab coats and take what we've learned from our past to craft our next attempt. We can zoom in to design the experiment with our best guess as to what might work for us. We can get specific and set a time limit so that we can focus on the task, and then zoom out after thirty days and ask, "Is this working for me?"

Finally, we know how important it is to ask the right questions and focus on tracking the right variable for us. Based on our detective work, we can decide if tracking calories or counting our steps is motivating or demotivating. We can ask if keeping track of a daily streak helps or harms our chance to change. We can take a risk and try something new, because we know it's just an experiment:

- "I am going to set aside thirty minutes each evening after the kids go to bed to work on a piece of art that makes me happy, and see how I feel at the end of the month."

- "I'm going to swap out half my regular sodas with sparkling water for the next month to see if this satisfies my need for fizzy drinks without the sugar and calories."
- "I'm going to sign up for a month of personal-trainer services to see if I can get excited about strength training, learn the moves, and decide if I like this more than exercise classes."

These experiments are very deliberate. They're not thirty-day sprints or shreds or detoxes. They're short experiments that we can zoom in and focus on, and then zoom out at the thirty-day mark and ask, "Is this working for me?" We can then decide if we need to tweak or change the experiment, or if we want to keep going.

When we apply a "curious scientist" mindset to life moving forward, we're moving from one experiment to the next without judgment. We're simply trying something to see if it works for us.

Sometimes our experiment turns out the way we hoped, and sometimes it turns out differently. Maybe we learn that we don't enjoy running or we dislike being in gyms. This is valuable information. Sometimes we learn that a low-carb diet works better for us than a low-fat diet or vice versa. Great!

The point isn't to "win," but to conduct a successful experiment. As long as we keep experimenting, even if some experiments fail, we give ourselves the best chance to find a path that fits our life and situation.

By the way, I bet you're surprised that in a book about experimentation and failure, I haven't quoted light bulb inventor Thomas Edison, who allegedly said, "I didn't fail. I simply found ten thousand ways that didn't work." Credit to me for not using that cliché quote. Instead, I'll leave you with one from Aaron Paul's character Jesse Pinkman in *Breaking Bad*: "Yeah, science!"

Key Insights

Solve the mystery of Past Us. It's time to research *why* our past attempts failed, but we're going to do so with the curiosity and focus of a detective. We're going to ask why enough times until we find out what's really going on. We know that what looks like a "lack of motivation" problem is usually a "resources" problem in disguise. This detective work gives us the best chance to do things differently next time.

Don't pick a goal; conduct an experiment. Goals are often vague: "I want to exercise more" or "I'm going to go on a diet." Instead, we're going to conduct an experiment like Marie Curie or Mr. Wizard. We form a hypothesis, we pick the experiment and a time frame, and then we find out if it's a good strategy or habit *for us.* We approach the experiment with curiosity, understanding that any outcome is a success, because it gives us important information.

Test the right variable. Show me the incentive, I'll show you the result. Maybe "lose weight fast" isn't the right metric to track for your health and well-being. Maybe "read fifty books this year" isn't going to have you reading for enjoyment or picking challenging books. Instead, let's pick something to track on a shorter time frame with sustainable results that feel manageable and allows for the unexpected chaos of life.

Zoom In, Zoom Out: When we conduct an experiment, we need to set the parameters, and then pick a date four to six weeks into the future and put it on our calendar. We can zoom in and commit to the experiment without expectation. And then, four to six weeks later, we can zoom out, evaluate the experiment, analyze the results, and decide if we want to change the experiment or keep going.

THE PACT FRAMEWORK

Pause

Accept

Change

Try

5

T IS FOR TRY

Start Ugly and Get Good

You admire a character for trying more than for their successes.

—Emma Coats, Pixar story artist

We've learned to pause, process, and not make things worse. We've learned to accept our reality with compassion, let go, and lean in.

We've learned to think about change differently and conduct a fun experiment instead of picking a boring goal.

With these three steps out of the way, it's time for us to learn the fourth step in the PACT:

Try.

We're not going to set sky-high expectations, make grand declarations, or burn the boats behind us and go all in. Instead, we're going to adjust our expectations and look at this next attempt to change like a beta test. We're trying something different. We can then decide what fits, how it fits, and where to go from there.

If we are willing to try, then we've already taken the most difficult step.

The next most important step is learning *how to try.* We'll learn from my three favorite forms of entertainment: the film industry, the video game industry, and stand-up comedy.

Let's nerd out.

When Trying Something New, Start Ugly

In 1973, a young writer-director, fresh off the unexpected success of his last film, began work on his next script. Every morning at 8 a.m., he would sit at his desk with a goal of writing five pages. He'd usually only have one page done by 4 p.m., and then he'd panic-write the final four pages over the next hour.

What was he working on?

A movie about aliens.

After an ugly first draft left his film friends befuddled, he rewrote the movie and made some major changes. The updated screenplay involved a villain with a laser sword who was very strong in the ways of "the Bogan." When he asked another friend for feedback, the reply was: "This is absolute gobbledygook."

You might not be a screenwriter, but "gobbledygook" isn't quite the feedback you're hoping for on a creative project.

So what is this nonsense movie we're talking about?

Its working title was *Adventures of the Starkiller*!

It was hopefully the first of many in a saga called *The Star*

Wars. Fortunately for us nerds, George Lucas kept at it, and after multiple rewrites, the screenplay started to take shape. By the time he wrote his third and fourth drafts, Luke Skywalker entered the story; Darth Vader, Chewie, Leia, and Obi-Wan all became fully realized.

And the rest is *Star Wars* history.

Okay. Actually, all sorts of things went wrong. The fact that this movie ever got made is a miracle. Multiple studios passed on it and most couldn't understand what the film was about (including most of the British crew and some of the actors on set!). The first winter rain in fifty years in Tunisia delayed the production almost immediately, and Lucas became so stressed out from the production he suffered anxiety attacks. Furthermore, Lucas parted ways with the film's original editor halfway through the editing process and brought in a new team that gave us the film we saw on screen, that won our hearts.

The more I studied screenplays and movies and origin stories, the more I uncovered comically bad first drafts and bizarre working titles. The working title for Ridley Scott's cult classic *Alien* was *Star Beast*. The original title for Pixar's *WALL-E*? *Trash Planet*. One producer wanted to rename *Back to the Future* "Space Men from Pluto." Great Scott, that's terrible!

We all have to start somewhere, and the scariest thing of all is to start with nothing. Which means we need to first be willing to do something poorly.

This requires a different kind of courage.

Sir Winston Churchill is not a person one would normally

associate with fear. Early in his career as a war journalist he was captured as a POW in the Boer War in South Africa and then escaped, calling it a "grand adventure." During World War I, he went to the front lines in France to get a better understanding of the battlefield. This is nothing compared to his World War II accomplishments.

I bring up Churchill's often reckless bravado to (literally) paint a comical contrast to how he approached art.

During his notorious "exile"[14] from His Majesty's government, Churchill wrote extensively and continued other pursuits, including landscape painting. Churchill shared his fear of staring at a blank canvas in his essay "Painting as a Pastime" about learning to paint:

> The next step was to begin. But what a step to take! The palette gleamed with beads of color; fair and white rose the canvas; the empty brush hung poised, heavy with destiny, irresolute in the air. My hand seemed arrested by a silent veto.

He was so afraid of making a mistake he couldn't get himself to put the paintbrush on the canvas. Fortunately, his wife, Clementine, had strategically invited Hazel Lavery, a neighbor and artist, to come by at that exact moment. According to William

---

14 He wasn't really exiled, but from 1929 to 1939, his positions against greater self-rule for India, supporting King Edward's abdication, and encouraging early arming against Nazi Germany made him politically radioactive.

Goldsmith in *The Last Lion: Volume 1*, she strode up to Churchill and his canvas and took charge:

> What are you hesitating about? Let me have a brush—the big one." She splashed it into turpentine, socked it into the blue and white, thrashed it about on the palette, and delivered several huge, savage strokes on what Winston called "the absolutely cowering canvas.

This is when Churchill discovered the canvas "could not hit back. No evil fate avenged the jaunty violence. The canvas grinned in helplessness before [him]. The spell was broken."

Which brings me to our next attempt, my friend. Anything worth doing is probably worth doing poorly at the start.

- We can't write a masterpiece without first writing a draft that's described as "gobbledygook."
- We can't play the violin beautifully without first making it sound like an asthmatic cat.
- We can't become a gourmet chef if we first don't burn a meal or two or ten.

Musician, actor, and comedian Donald Glover told *The New York Times* that nobody on their deathbed looks back and is happy they avoided embarrassment by trying something new. (Okay, he actually used the phrase "avoided being cringe," but I'm not cool enough to say that, so I paraphrased.)

Trying can be scary. Being *seen* trying is downright terrifying.

If you're worried about feeling embarrassed to try something new, I have two publicly embarrassing moments that I'm proud to share with you.

After getting cut from my high school basketball team (mostly because I sucked at basketball), I joined Sportsite, the only gym in my hometown of Sandwich, Massachusetts. On my first day in the gym, trying to stay under the radar, I did the exact opposite. I walked immediately to the bench, loaded forty-five-pound weights on either side of the barbell, and decided to try bench presses.

Mind you, I probably weighed 120 pounds at this point. And yet, as my spaghetti arms struggled to lift the weight off the safety supports, never once did I think, "Maybe this is too much weight."

The next ten seconds played out like a scene from a 1980s coming-of-age movie.

I immediately dropped the bar onto my rib cage, panicked, and did the only thing I could: I rolled the bar over my ribcage to the left and watched as the weight spun off the bar and crashed onto the floor. BANG! Of course, the bar now had forty-five pounds on only one side, so that side shot down toward the floor. BANG! For extra embarrassment, this was up on the second floor, so every single person could see or hear my catastrophe.

I put the bar back on the rack and then sat up to see dozens of eyes staring at me.

So, no matter how your first day goes in the gym, as long as you don't cave in your chest and almost kill yourself, you're already light-years ahead of young Steve!

But wait! There's more.

Years later, I filmed my first video for Nerd Fitness about doing a beginner body-weight workout. That video has now been viewed 1.5 million times. It's the most popular YouTube video on our channel by a long shot. That video also includes me wearing my shorts backward, which I didn't realize until five hundred thousand views later.

So, as long as you can put your clothes on the right way, you're already off to a better start with your YouTube or social media presence.

Whatever we try, eventually we'll look back on our early efforts with embarrassment. That's actually a great sign: It means we cared enough and got better at it.

As artist and author David duChemin laments, most people are so afraid of doing something poorly, they never start.

His advice for anybody embarking on a new mission also happens to be the name of one of his books:

Start ugly.

Ready, FIRE, Aim: The Art of Hilarious Improvement

Every night in tiny rooms around the world, brave souls take the most dangerous stage of all: open mic night at comedy clubs. These gladiators fail more often than not, in truly hilarious fashion.

Once we overcome our fear of starting ugly, we can channel stand-up comics and get to work being less bad.

Prussian general Helmuth von Moltke the Elder once said that no plan survives contact with the enemy. Similarly in comedy, no joke survives contact with the audience.

Comics don't tell a joke *because* it's funny.
They tell a joke *until* it's funny.

A joke begins as an anecdote or an observation. It's a "best guess" at something that *might* be funny. It's a shout into the void, often accompanied by "Is this anything?" That first day telling a joke is usually *painful*. Nobody laughs, and the comedian awkwardly follows it up with "Okay, guess that's not ready."

The next time they tell that joke, they tell it slightly differently with a new punch line. Again, crickets.

But the third time they tell it, they get *one* chuckle. That comedian now has their first win, and they can start to build on that joke. The next time they tell it, it gets a bit funnier, and they get a few more laughs.

And from there, one adjustment or tweak at a time, a comedy set gets built. That's what makes stand-up so darn impressive. It's a meticulously crafted performance made to look effortless. As comedian Mike Birbiglia told Scott Galloway on *The Prof G Pod*:

> You have to outthink your audience, and then make it seem like you're not outthinking your audience, and then you deliver as if it's this thing you just thought of, that's sort of the magic trick of it.

Every pause, every inflection, every "random" aside? It's all finely tuned based on crowd feedback, and dozens of experiments across dozens of sets.

Ask any comedian how to build a "tight five" (five-minute routine), and they'll tell you to find an open mic *tonight*, get on stage, and absolutely bomb. And then do the same tomorrow. And every night for the next thirty days. That's how a joke gets better: one painful attempt after another.

I saw comedian Taylor Tomlinson perform at the Ryman in 2023. This set was the finished product of twelve-plus months of carefully crafted anecdotes that had been told every night in comedy clubs across America. As chronicled by *The New York Times*, she closed with a story about her friend who got engaged but was afraid to tell Tomlinson.

Why?

As she tells it, her friend was being "so sweet and so hurtful" for making sure Tomlinson, recently single, was in a healthy headspace to hear about her friend's relationship happiness. Six months later, that line had evolved slightly into "I have never felt so seen and so insulted" because it got more laughs.

At one point Tomlinson even tested out different names for her friend's fiancé, all for the joke. A disdainfully delivered "TODD" got the biggest laugh. Each word, pause, name, and punch line, honed over months, based on feedback, created the end result that can now be seen on Netflix.

You might be thinking, "That's great, Steve, but what if I never plan on telling a joke?"

I got you covered. This exact same "ready, fire, aim" strategy is how every Pixar film gets made too.

As Ed Catmull, cofounder of Pixar, likes to say, "Pixar films are not good at first, and our job is to make them so—to go, as I say, 'from suck to not-suck.'"

They're not afraid to start ugly and then adjust, based on feedback from "the Brain trust," a trusted group of problem-solvers within the company who provide critical guidance to early films.

For the film *Up*, director Pete Docter first envisioned a movie about two spoiled princes in a floating castle who fell down to earth. The Brain Trust couldn't relate to the princes and struggled to understand the rules of the floating castle.

The next version kept only two things from the first pass—a floating dwelling and a funny bird—but now included an old man named Carl. It was in the third version that the trip to Venezuela was added, and in the fourth version Docter finally nailed the message and the plot. *Up* had to go through these changes and incorporate feedback to uncover the groundbreaking final version of the film that makes us laugh and cry.

Pixar films are always a "best first guess," followed by thoughtful feedback, and then a "next best guess," done repeatedly. Sometimes, their guesses are way off, and much of their work must be discarded. From Pixar's perspective, though, that's simply the cost of trying new things.

They don't know their final destination, so they "get in the neighborhood" and explore a few roads, even if some of those roads require them to turn back. They know that all of this is helpful knowledge and useful information that will help inform future trips.

No matter what we're trying to accomplish, we can still *think* like stand-up comics and Pixar creators.

Spending months crafting the perfect plan is doing ourselves a disservice compared with crafting a simple strategy and starting ugly.

We're not launching rockets or building a submarine here.

We're just trying to create a workout schedule that works for us. We're trying to change how we eat. We're trying to learn the piano or how to juggle.

We're much better off treating change like an ugly first draft. We can look for early wins that show what we're doing is working. We can also ask for feedback or guidance to find out what's not working.

That's what most of life is: a "best first guess" followed by feedback (internal and external), and then an adjustment. It's how we end up in new, interesting places.

We might go to the gym expecting to get toned in a cardio class, but discover that we love feeling strong when we pick up heavy weights.

We might start writing historical fiction about the staff at an English castle, only to realize that our test readers aren't loving it. We can pivot a few details and turn it into time-traveling romantasy.

We might start making instructional videos about physics, but realize we have much more fun when we make videos nerding out about Magic: The Gathering.

If we're open to seeing the flashing lights and signals life sends our way as we try new experiments, really interesting things can happen.

Not to get too "meta," but this book in your hands has gone through twenty drafts.

I started with a series of random anecdotes and stories that had been popular essays with my audience. It took me four months to write the first draft, which was about 120,000 words of chaos (the book you are reading is fewer than 70,000 words).

I then spent two years making it better, cutting out the parts that didn't work, and sending occasional ugly drafts to my own Brain Trust (my editor Pete and my friends Baker, Matt, Eric, Jack, Jodi, and Mike).

Each version got less and less bad.

I specifically asked them to tell me which parts didn't work. This was *excruciating*, but I had to reframe my mindset to think "this is valuable feedback" and not an attack on me personally! I had to check my ego. I had to "kill my darlings" as author Stephen King would say. I had to learn to take feedback.

And twenty versions later, we have *How to Try Again*!

(See, I told you I'm not just the author, I'm also a client.)

"Get Good": Win or Learn

Author Brandon Sanderson tells aspiring writers to remind themselves: "I can do hard things. Doing hard things has intrinsic value, and they will make me a better person, even if I end up failing." When we decide to do hard things, it teaches us a lot about ourselves. And as long as we've learned something from that attempt, it's never a waste of time or effort.

I learned this valuable life lesson in the most unlikely of places.

By the mid-2000s, video games had leveled up from a hobby for nerds to mainstream entertainment. As the audience for gaming exploded, and as technology made gaming more immersive, so came larger teams, longer development cycles, and much higher costs.

The potential for financial success was equaled by the potential for fiscal ruin. Investors and boards of directors wanted their investment protected, asking developers to do whatever possible to make sure gamers never got too frustrated or overwhelmed.

In 2011, one company went *hard* in the other direction.

Instead of holding the gamer's hand, Japanese developer FromSoftware opted for minimal instruction, *no* guidance, and punishing difficulty. They dropped the player in the middle of a devastating landscape full of dragons, undead warriors, and grotesque monsters with a simple "Good luck, idiot!"

What started out as a "game for hardcore gamers" developed a cult following and would go on to critical and financial success, fundamentally changing the video game landscape forever. It was later recognized at the 2021 Golden Joystick Awards as the Ultimate Game of All Time. It spawned multiple sequels (and spiritual successors) that have sold over 60 million copies, and even became its own video game genre.

If you're a gamer, you probably know I'm talking about *Dark Souls*.[15] I assumed these games weren't for me, but nearly a decade after its release, I finally took a chance and tried it out.

---

15 Yes, I know, *Demon's Souls* came first, but *Dark Souls* was the breakout star.

And yep, *Dark Souls* is difficult.

But as its creator Hidetaka Miyazaki told *The New Yorker*, the game's difficulty is a feature, not a bug: "In our games specifically, hardship is what gives meaning to the experience."

Speaking from my time with *Dark Souls*, that's 100 percent accurate.

I have never felt a more satisfying joy (or had a more elevated heart rate) than when defeating a difficult *Dark Souls* boss. The game teaches the player that things will get more difficult, but the player *will* also get stronger and develop the skills to handle more adversity. This is our "Yes, and" philosophy of acceptance in action: "Yes, this game is hard, and here's how I will get better."

Paradoxically, *Dark Souls* becomes more addicting *because* we know we're going to die repeatedly. Each failure teaches a lesson. Each death creates excitement and momentum to try again *differently*. Each new run is a chance to change tactics, to learn a new attack pattern, or to go level up elsewhere and come back stronger.

There's this term popularized in gaming communities around *Dark Souls* and its difficulty:

You just have to "get good."[16]

Let's talk about our next "try" in life. We will try something until we find a path that works, and then we'll try something else when it stops working. Eventually, we get good, and then we will try something else.

---

16 Sometimes, it's spelled "git gud" because gamers can't help themselves.

Over the past few years as I navigated one failure after another, I kept stumbling across the phrase "You win or you learn."

Although it's been attributed to everybody from Kobe Bryant to mixed martial arts coach John Cavanagh, its origins allegedly go back even further, to Carlos Gracie, the dude who developed the martial art of Brazilian jiu-jitsu:

"There is no losing in jiu-jitsu. You either win or you learn."

Of course, losing still hurts sometimes. It just hurts less when there's also meaning to our struggle and a lesson to learn in the loss.

We win or we learn. And eventually, we get good.

No Matter What You Try, Pre-Accept Any Outcome

We've spent this chapter talking about trying differently.

I've spent very little time on outcomes and expectations, because that's the *last* piece of the puzzle. It's also the one fraught with the most baggage.

When we *need* a specific outcome to happen, especially when the outcome isn't within our control, that's the fastest path to paralysis (and never trying) or perpetual disappointment (when it doesn't work out):

Needing to "write a wildly successful book" is the best way to fill ourselves with enough anxiety to never write, or write a book so bland that it appeals to nobody.

Needing to hit a certain number on the scale is the only guaranteed way to make sure we always feel "less than" for every day we're not at that weight.

Needing to receive a certain amount of recognition or have a certain number of followers or readers or fans guarantees we'll never be satisfied or feel like we're enough.

I want to share my favorite tactic on reframing expectations from somebody who teaches this very skill as his job.

Josh Nichols has competed at the highest levels of amateur golf, finishing runner-up at the 2017 US Mid-Amateur tournament. He's now a performance coach and host of the *Mental Golf Show* podcast.

I shared a personal struggle with Josh that plagued me for years: Whenever I started to play a good round of golf (scoring well), it would make me so nervous and uncomfortable that I would fall apart and have a few terrible holes. I knew I had the skill to play well. Unfortunately, desperately hoping to continue playing well all but guaranteed I would inevitably fall apart.

I asked Josh how he manages to stay focused and present when he has a chance to shoot a really low score. His answer caught me off guard.

He explained that so much of golf is out of our control. More often than not, the ball will not go exactly where we want it to. It's not the course's fault, or the ball's fault, or the club's fault. Josh has no expectation for things to happen a certain way, because that's just part of the game.

Instead, he lets go of the outcome and commits to being

present. Before each shot, he tells himself, "I pre-accept any outcome," and then hits the ball without expectation.

I was skeptical.

To play well . . . I have to deliberately STOP trying to play well?

But I trusted Josh, and his proven track record of success spoke for itself. So I tried it just a few days later, in a friendly tournament with the *Chasing Scratch* podcast community. Before each shot, I had a little mantra to free my brain from anxiety and expectation: "I pre-accept any outcome. Golf is fun. Good vibes only. Let's go."

It was silly, but it got me out of my head, kept me present, and reminded me that I was playing golf with friends, something I love doing. Like a scene out of a sports movie, I shot my best score ever. Even better, my teammate (shout-out to Brady Shark) and I won our division!

I had to *let go of the expectation of playing well* to play well.

Learning to let go will apply to the rest of our lives.

When we find ourselves paralyzed by needing a specific outcome, we must get out of our own way long enough to just do the damn thing. To do the workout. To pick up the paintbrush. To cook the next meal. To write the next book.

To give our best effort, we need to pre-accept whatever outcome might happen, good, bad, or ugly. If we commit to doing the thing with our full attention, that's really all we can ask of ourselves. If the outcome is out of our control, all we can focus on is our effort.

We can start ugly. We can find the courage to be seen trying.
We can take a best guess, and then adjust based on feedback.
We can pre-accept any outcome.
And if that outcome ends up being something unexpected?
It's not a loss. It's a lesson.
We win or we learn.
And we get good.

Key Insights

Start ugly. It's so easy to put pressure on ourselves to perform well immediately that we never start. What a shame. The only way to go from "suck to not-suck" is to be okay launching our first experiment out into the void. We cannot edit a blank page or improve an unwritten song.

Ready, FIRE, aim. No battle plan survives contact with the enemy, and no joke survives contact with the audience. Life is going to provide us with all sorts of feedback, so we need to keep our eyes and ears open for the lessons life is trying to teach us, and be open to making adjustments.

Get good: You win or you learn. We are capable of doing hard things, and even if we don't succeed, we will still learn a lesson along the way. Like trying to survive in *Dark Souls*, every failure teaches a lesson and every attempt is an opportunity to try again differently. Over time, with enough persistence, we get good.

Pre-accept any outcome. We can commit to our next experiment, but we cannot guarantee its outcome. Putting MORE emphasis on the expected result is one of the fastest ways to making sure that result is never achieved. By pre-accepting any outcome, we can get out of our own head and focus on the experiment itself.

PACT RECAP

CONGRATULATIONS! We now have a functional philosophy we can take with us through the rest of life. I have some more advanced strategies and guides in the following chapters on how to implement this framework in other parts of life, but let's first begin with a recap of how we got here.

We have a better understanding for what to do when we fail at something or feel stuck. We can forgive ourselves for being human. We can thank Past Us for getting us this far, and say "I can take it from here."

The PACT Framework

We can **PAUSE** and give ourselves the mental bandwidth to process what's really going on. Like Brett Archibald stranded in the Indian Ocean, as soon as we realize we're swimming against the current, we stop making things worse. Next, we remove the expectations we've placed on our shoulders to juggle everything and narrow our focus to just treading water. Instead of trying to win, we make sure we don't lose. Whether it's taking a short walk or doing a five-minute workout, we are signaling to ourselves "I'm still here," and that counts.

Next, we can **ACCEPT** reality. This includes recognizing the "back to normal" fallacy, and accepting that our messy lives are normal. Instead of trying to catch up on everything and optimize everything, we finally accept that this is an impossible task. Only by letting go and giving up can we finally start to make progress on the stuff that matters. We can open Pandora's box and lean into the uncomfortable lesson that life is trying to teach us. And finally we can embrace "Yes, and" thinking: "Yes, this situation is unfair, and here's how I'm choosing to spend my time."

Third, we'll remember that we must **CHANGE** something. We remember the adage: If we always do what we've always done, we'll always get what we've always got. We can look back on our past like detectives to see how we struggled and what didn't work. We can then decide, like scientists, which experiment we'd like to try next, and which metric we'll be tracking. We can zoom in to focus on our experiment, and then zoom out and ask without judgment, "Is this working for me?"

Finally, we can **TRY** again, with the expectation that we're going to start ugly. If we can embrace the "ready, FIRE, aim" art of improvement like stand-up comics, we can make a best guess and then improve along the way thanks to feedback. Finally, we can challenge ourselves to do hard things, because even if we don't succeed, we've still learned a valuable lesson. We know there's no such thing as wasted effort: We either win or we learn. We can commit to the task without expectations, pre-accept any outcome, and eventually "get good."

Part Two

HOW TO USE PACTS IN OUR LIVES

Welcome to Part Two, my friend.

If I've done my job right, you're finding fun ways to wedge PACT into any conversation. Thanks for that. But I don't want to just send you off on your merry way and say, "Good luck!"

I want to talk about what to do with our next attempt, our next experiment, our next use of PACT.

I'd love to tell you that now everything gets easier.

But that's not how life works! Life will probably get busier and more complicated, and more things will go off the rails. Not because we've done anything wrong, but because on a long enough timeline, anything that might happen will happen.

Which is fine, because that's what keeps life interesting.

That's why we have five more important chapters to cover.

Think of these chapters like a buffet where you get to pick which part of the journey you're most focused on right now. My hope is that you can return to whichever chapter you need whenever life happens to require it.

We'll start with **Chapter 6: How to Pick the Next Thing to Try.** Every day we hear about the next great "thing": a new workout or diet or optimization strategy that promises to solve all our problems. How do we decide which ones are worthy of the hype and which are a waste of time? I thought you'd never ask.

This chapter will help develop the right mindset to pick our next "thing," grade ourselves on the right scorecard, and not get sucked into chasing the wrong goal.

Chapter 7: Escape the Doom Loop: How to Protect Yourself from Yourself will cover all the fun ways we will sabotage ourselves on our journey. Specifically, how we often set unrealistic expectations, go all in, and then give up when life happens. I'll share some crucial "Escape Pods" we can hop in when we find ourselves falling back into this negative, self-critical Doom Loop. Not that any of us do that.

Next, **Chapter 8: How to Keep Doing the Thing** is full of practical strategies that *might* help us stay committed on the next experiment we attempt. Although nothing in life is a guarantee, I bet at least one of these tactics will be helpful. These are some of my favorite methods for habit and routine building that my team and I have been teaching since 2009.

But then there's the late Act Two plot twist. Life is random and unfair, so there will come a point when a surprise shows up uninvited. Luckily, I've got you covered here too.

Chapter 9: When Life Kicks Your Ass, Here's What to Do is about how to avoid devastation when needing to process unfair life experiences for us or our loved ones. This is the "break glass in case of emergency" chapter to help keep us from falling into true despair, whether we're navigating an injury, illness, or an event that permanently changes what life looks like.

And finally, we'll round things out with **Chapter 10: How to Navigate Life with Flexible Resilience.** I'll explain how to take the PACT framework and apply it over months, years, and decades to navigate life's various ups and downs. This chapter will be a bit more philosophical and operate at a higher altitude, but I promise to keep things interesting.

I haven't let you down yet, right?

6

HOW TO PICK THE NEXT THING TO TRY

When one does the next and most necessary thing without fuss and with conviction, one always does what is meaningful and intended by fate.

—Carl Jung

It's finally time to decide which "thing" we'll spend our time and energy working on next.

Do we dive right into the latest trendy diet?

Do we follow the optimized morning routine of our favorite podcaster?

Do we take our clothes off and go streaking through the quad to the gymnasium?

Maybe! But probably not.

One of the fastest ways to guarantee future failure is to pick the wrong strategy for the wrong reason.

And boy, is that an easy trap to fall into. Every day, we're bombarded with yet another miracle solution to all our problems, whether it's a new supplement, diet, or optimized routine. How the heck do we decide? And once we decide, what if *something better comes along?*

Fortunately, I'm going to go over a filtering strategy we can apply to every future book, product, diet, video, or podcast we stumble across in our quest to live healthier or happier.

When our brain tells us to get overly excited and chase the shiny new object, when we're suddenly faced with conflicting lifestyle choices from two equally charismatic influencers, we need a personal philosophy that helps us decide confidently while ignoring the hype and noise.

Life will always be busy and there will always be a new fancy-pants strategy begging for our attention (and our hard-earned money). Our normal will only continue to get weirder.

If we can keep our focus on what's important to us, if we can accept that there's no magic solution that will solve our problems, we can learn to put our efforts toward stuff that *actually* works.

We already have enough on our plate, so let's build a plan that follows our PACT framework.

There's No "Right Way" to Change

Neal Stephenson is the best-selling author of some of the best science fiction novels ever written. I remember stumbling across an essay he wrote, "Why I Am a Bad Correspondent," where he explained why he was unavailable to reply to every email and attend every engagement he gets invited to.

> Writing novels is hard, and requires vast, unbroken slabs of time. Four quiet hours is a resource that I can put to

> good use. Two slabs of time, each two hours long, might add up to the same four hours, but are not nearly as productive as an unbroken four. . . . The productivity equation is a non-linear one, in other words.

Aspiring authors might read that and think, "I need four hours of unbroken time or I will never get my writing done." If you're a new parent, you work a full-time job, and you suddenly find yourself caring for an ailing parent, you might lose hope and say, "I'll never find the time to write my book."

All right, let's look at another writing strategy.

Ian Fleming was a former British Naval Intelligence officer and author of the James Bond novels. Each winter, Fleming would fly to Jamaica and stay at his private oceanfront compound, Goldeneye. There he followed a strict routine: He would wake up at sunrise, and write each morning from 9 a.m. to noon on a gold-plated typewriter. He would swim, lunch, nap, and then edit from 4 p.m. to 6 p.m. before crushing cocktails. This was done like clockwork each winter. The result was twelve novels and two short stories in fourteen years.

What, you *don't* have a private Jamaican compound or a gold-plated typewriter? *AND* you have a family and a child with special needs and a job and other responsibilities? Oh well, I guess that's the end of your ambition.

Okay, fine, let me share one more example.

Agatha Christie is the author of sixty-six detective novels and fifteen short story collections that have sold *two billion* copies worldwide.

This is slightly more copies than I have sold (so far).

When asked how she was able to write so prolifically, one would imagine a situation like Neal Stephenson: a dedicated, quiet workspace and a completely empty calendar with large blocks of uninterrupted time.

Her response will surprise you. As she shared in *Agatha Christie: An Autobiography*:

> I was enjoying myself so much in ordinary living that writing was a task which I performed in spells and bursts. I never had a definite place which was my room or where I retired specially to write.
>
> . . . Many friends have said to me, "I never know when you write your books, because I've never seen you writing, or even seen you go away to write."
>
> I must behave rather as dogs do when they retire with a bone; they depart in a secretive manner and you do not see them again for an odd half hour.

Yep, this is the exact opposite strategy from Stephenson and Fleming. Yet she still somehow wrote dozens of incredibly fun and successful books in this manner.

So, which of these tactics is *best?*

Which one creates optimal results?

They all work . . . for the right person.

Each author discovered a routine and style that worked *for them.* Any one of them would flounder if they tried to follow the writing routine of another person.

Personally, I would struggle to get any writing done if I lived on a private Jamaican compound with the Caribbean outside the window. I asked my publisher to buy me a Jamaican writing compound for testing purposes.[17]

Whether it's a writing strategy, a morning routine, a workout or diet, a painting technique, or learning how to talk to strangers, most strategies will probably work, if we actually do them. And that's where people get in trouble.

Let's not chase a strategy that creates the "optimal" results.

Instead, let's pick a strategy that we can follow pretty consistently, most of the time, for a long time:

- The best diet is the one we *actually* stick with.
- The best time to work out is when *we can actually work out.*
- The best parenting style is the *one that works for us and our family.*

Many people search for the optimal without ever bothering to ask, "Do I see myself actually following through with this?"

17 They said no.

Remember, things like eating food, exercising and trying to make positive changes in our lives are all lifelong experiments.

We can't really "cram" for them like a test and then be "done."

Permanent progress requires permanent change, which means we need to pick changes that we can *actually* stick with for months, years, or decades.

Making small changes to our how we eat regularly (eating one less snack per day and adding more fruit to our diet) will create slower progress than crash dieting and giving up carbs for a month. But it might be something we can actually stick with for years, because it allows us the freedom to eat fast food without guilt when it's our weekend with the kids.

If we write a few hundred words each morning before the kids wake up, it will take longer to write a book than if we move to a cabin in the woods and drink enough caffeine to levitate. But it's more likely to result in us building a long-term writing habit that fits into our hectic life. Also I've seen enough horror movies to be wary of cabins in the woods.

The most optimal, the fastest, or the most efficient solution might be the one we quickly abandon because it makes us miserable. If we can't wait to be done with our new diet, then it's not the diet for us. If we are counting down the days until we don't have to go to boot-camp class, it's not the style of exercise for us!

There are an infinite number of paths to make progress on whatever experiment we choose, but it does require us to compassionately accept the constraints of our life. It also requires us to do some soul-searching to understand why we want to change in the first place.

Make Sure You Know the Rules You're Following

On his *Money for Couples* podcast, Ramit Sethi interviews couples who are fighting over car payments and Target shopping sprees. They *think* they're arguing about budgets, but it goes so much deeper than dollars and cents. This is why Ramit asks them, "What was your parents' relationship with money like?" Some guests grew up wealthy but are terrified to spend money, while other guests spend frivolously even if they're in extreme debt. These behaviors are often a result of learned behavior, aren't logical, and can go unnoticed for decades.

Sethi refers to these behaviors as "invisible scripts," deeply held beliefs that dictate why we feel or behave a certain way, often without realizing it.

If we look closely, we can see these rules everywhere: how we dress, how we act on dates, how we treat money, how we do our jobs, how we raise our children, how we think about exercise.

They even apply to our relationship with food.

For example, did you grow up hearing "You have to clean your plate," even if you were already full and not hungry?

We can thank Herbert Hoover for that.

During the tumultuous year of 1917, it was believed that "food will win [World War I]."

President Woodrow Wilson asked Herbert Hoover, head of the U.S. Food Administration, to decrease the nation's food consumption and waste. This would free up more food to be shipped over to Europe to feed the soldiers on the front lines.

So Hoover created the Clean Plate Club and had households sign pledge cards like:

> At the table I'll not leave a scrap of food upon my plate.
> And I'll not eat between meals, but for supper time I'll wait.

The government encouraged people to reduce food waste by putting less food on their plates, but making sure to eat all of it. Every wasted meal was one less meal that could have been sent to feed soldiers in Europe.

This is how "clean your plate" became a catchphrase that appeared in hundreds of posters across the country. It also became ingrained in an entire generation of Americans, who had to go through the Great Depression a short while later. It's probably why our grandparents told our parents to clean their plates: It was a matter of survival for a large chunk of their lives.

And that's why our parents, who might have grown up with some food insecurity, said the same thing to us as kids.

You might not have had the Clean Plate Club in your house, but I bet there were other unspoken rules. Maybe you were one of ten kids and food *was* scarce. Maybe your single dad worked three jobs and expressed his love through bringing home fast food. Maybe your mom ate low-fat microwave meals and brought you to Weight Watchers as a seven-year-old.

No matter how much of an independent thinker we think we are, there are still decades of stories and invisible rules that have impacted our relationship with food, money, exercise, politics, and how we treat ourselves.

No wonder change is so hard and complicated.

There's reality, and then there's the story we tell ourselves about reality that shapes our behavior.

So, before we pick "the thing" to do next, let's get curious about why we're picking it in the first place.

We can decide which stories or rules or beliefs are still serving us, which ones need to be updated, and which ones should be launched into the sun.

Maybe we don't need to clean our plate, particularly when we're trying to heal our relationship with food. Learning to stop when we're full could be a life-changing skill we develop.

Maybe we don't need to treat financial success as the key to happiness, particularly when our dad did the same thing, and it contributed to the end of his relationship with Mom.

Maybe we don't need to continue the family tradition of avoiding uncomfortable conversations, or always yelling, or not respecting boundaries.

Just because it's "always been done this way" doesn't mean we need to keep doing it that way. Only after letting go of rules that don't fit can we make room for new rules and beliefs and stories that are uniquely ours.

Once we start to sort out what's best for us, we can confidently ignore the things that are no longer serving us.

How Do You Define "Success"? Grade Yourself on *Your* Scorecard.

I love watching documentaries about amazing things I have absolutely no desire to do.

My heart skipped two beats watching the Academy Award–winning documentary *Free Solo* about climber Alex Honnold scaling El Capitan in Yosemite National Park *without a safety rope*. I'll stick with my safe indoor rock climbing walls, thank you.

The Rescue, a documentary about the cave-diving volunteers who rescued the trapped Thai boys soccer team restored my faith in humanity. I was a blubbering mess by the end. At the same time, the mere idea of diving through underwater caves fills me with dread and is something you couldn't pay me to do.

I love watching incredible people doing incredible things like this, while also appreciating that I never have to do those things.

Unfortunately, that reasonable mentality does *not* apply when I learn about things I *kind of* want to do, or *think* I could do. This is where I get myself into trouble.

It's unsexy to accept that success in *anything* requires sacrifices in other areas of life. That's not what the folks selling us the dream want us to believe. They need to convince us that as long as we live like them (and buy their product or service), we can be successful too. No compromises required!

We see a financially successful entrepreneur telling us to rise and grind. We don't see that person working late nights at the office to avoid their family (because they are fighting with their spouse), their deep insecurities, or the void they're trying to fill with more money.

We see the perfect family living on a farmstead in Wyoming, or living out of a van on the road, bragging about the amazingness of life "off the grid." We don't see the loneliness, the lack of deep community connections, or the eventual challenges their kids could face because Mom and Dad plastered their personal lives all over social media before they had a chance to consent.

We see the super-shredded celebrity telling us how they got fit for a film in six months. We don't see the two trainers, the dietitian, the private chef, the nanny taking care of their child, or the millions of dollars at stake dependent on them looking superficially healthy.[18]

By the way, there's nothing wrong with these people doing these things: They are doing so for their own reasons, with their own motivations. Everybody gets to live their own life. Many of these people are actually happy, while many of them are secretly miserable. The truth is that we can never truly know.

---

18 Performance-enhancing substances are often used as well, but we can't talk about that!

But problems arise when we take *our* life, *our* motivations, and *our* expectations, and compare them to others who are playing with a different scorecard.

We humans are social creatures. We love learning how to be successful or happy or healthy by copying others who we hope have all the answers. When we see somebody that has what we *think* we want, it's alluring to assume they found the one correct path and live a blissful life without any problems.

This is what's called "survivorship bias" in action: We only hear about the "super strategies" of the highly successful, and we don't hear about all the people who followed those exact strategies and burned out or went into ruin chasing the same dreams. Those people don't usually get book deals or TV shows.

Fortunately, there are plenty of celebrities and successful folks who are willing to give honest answers about their privilege, luck, and the severe trade-offs and sacrifices they've had to make. To paraphrase author Mark Manson, there's no such thing as a life without problems, only a life with different problems.

Comedian Bo Burnham was once asked on a late-night TV show how to succeed like him in life. His answer was honest:

> Don't take advice from people like me who have gotten very lucky. We're very biased. You know, like Taylor Swift[19] telling you to follow your dreams is

---

19 Before you get mad, I once shared an elevator with Taylor Swift, and she was delightful. Also, "Blank Space" is my favorite pop song from the past twenty years. Please don't come at me, Swifties!

like a lottery winner telling you, "Liquidize your assets. Buy Powerball tickets. It works."

I really appreciated this honest answer from Ken Burns, arguably the most accomplished documentarian alive. He's known for his award-winning documentaries about the Civil War, country music, Vietnam, baseball, and more. I am in awe of his ability to distill thousands of hours of interviews and archival footage into the ten most definitive hours on that topic.

Wanting to know more of his secret, I listened to his interview on the *SmartLess* podcast.

The hosts asked Burns how he managed to be so prolific and still keep a healthy work-life balance. He replied, "You'll have to ask my two ex-wives about that."

The cost of chasing greatness or trying to reach a level of performance might require more sacrifices than you or I am willing to make. That's okay.

Artist Austin Kleon has said on his popular blog for creatives: "Everybody wants to be the noun without doing the verb." Or in the immortal words of bodybuilder Ronnie Coleman: "Everybody wanna be a bodybuilder, don't nobody wanna lift no heavy-ass weight."

There's nothing wrong with admitting to ourselves that we don't actually want to do the work and make the sacrifices for the *chance* at some level of arbitrary success.[20]

---

20 This doesn't even consider the fact that so much of "success" comes down to blind luck, privilege, money, genetics, geography, social determinants of health, and other factors.

Many want to *have written a book*, but most don't want the daily drudgery of agonizing over a keyboard, maybe for years, writing and then editing and then re-editing what they've written.

Many want to *have run a marathon*, but most don't want to get up to train at 5 a.m. every day and then deal with shin splints and chafing (in all the wrong places) and deformed toenails from pounding the pavement for months.

Many want to *have washboard abs*, but most aren't willing to say no to all joyful food or beverages for months and years to reach a low enough body fat percentage that makes abs visible (and which still won't make them happy).

The problem isn't that we don't have the dedication required. It's that we have the expectation that we *should* have that dedication or be willing to make those sacrifices. It's perfectly okay that we don't want those things.

If we look at other people, who happen to be playing a *completely* different game from the one we're playing, and grade ourselves on their scorecard, we set ourselves up for disaster.

That's the fastest path to misery: chasing the wrong thing, following advice from the wrong person, with the wrong expectation, assuming it will finally make us happy or solve our problems.

When we encounter videos or interviews or success stories, we can pause and challenge our thoughts.

Instead of only asking "Is the juice worth the squeeze?" we should also ask "Do I actually *like* juice?"

This is something I struggled with for a good chunk of my career.

I tried turning Nerd Fitness into a big business because "that's what successful people do" only to realize that it brought me more stress than fulfillment. It made me miserable, and it came at the expense of the one part of my job that I loved: writing.

I chased this path for five years before finally admitting I was playing life on the wrong scorecard, chasing the wrong goal. It seems obvious in retrospect, but I never allowed myself to ask, "What if this actually works? Do I even want what's on the other side?"

When I hear the stories of other far more successful entrepreneurs, I still sometimes feel envy or jealousy. I have to constantly remind myself that I am not them. I haven't lived their life. I don't have their insecurities or motivations. My brain doesn't work the way theirs works. I don't want to make the sacrifices they've made. I don't even know if they're really happy or not.

I remind myself that sometimes, the juice isn't worth the squeeze.

And sometimes, I don't even want juice.

Choose the Right Thing for Us, Right Now

I don't know if you're going to pick a 5K running program or sign up for a writing workshop or learn to juggle. I don't know if you're looking to start dating, you want to become a better parent, or you're trying to work up the courage to go to your first open mic night.

No matter what you pick, as long as you've picked something that aligns with your values and the rules you live by, and is something *you* want, then you've already won.

You know *why* you're picking the thing.

You have realistic expectations about the thing.

You know what you're hoping to get by doing the thing.

You also understand what you're sacrificing to get the thing.

In other words, you are building your own buffet plate. I realize that sounds like an absurd statement that makes no sense, but let me explain.

In my early twenties, I worked for a company called Sixthman, which produces floating festivals on cruise ships in the Caribbean. Imagine thirty artists and bands performing across six venues on a big ship with two thousand die-hard fans. Some cruises are for Southern rock fans, while others are for fans of pop, punk, bluegrass, or Americana/folk.

I didn't get paid much, but damn, was it fun.

While on these cruises, part of my job was to host flip-cup tournaments, and interview bands, and make sure guests and artists alike had fun.

When I wasn't hosting events, the rest of my job involved checking in with guests to see how their vacation was going and if we could do anything for them. Which meant I had a *lot* of time to do some epic people-watching.

And there's no better place for people-watching than the cruise ship buffet.

These are massive rooms with fifteen food stations, each with a different theme. There are Tex-Mex options next to Asian fusion; there's a salad station next to the soft-serve ice cream machine.

It's a cornucopia of calories. A variety of vittles. A plethora of plates.

But I digest. *(Thought I had given up on the bad jokes, did ya?)*

Every day on these cruises, I witnessed two thousand people on vacation eating the most bizarre combinations of food.

I give you all of this setup for an absurd thought experiment.

Imagine you are on the Rock Boat (Sixthman's most famous event) and you haven't eaten all day. You enter the buffet line and start making your plate: chicken parmesan and garlic bread, some grilled veggies with shredded cheese, a bowl of Froot Loops, a mai-tai cocktail, and a piece of chocolate lava cake.

And then I show up.

I grab the plate of food from somebody else and swap it with yours. I then tell you how great this new plate of food is. It has a big serving of refried beans, even though you don't like refried beans. You are staring down at shrimp cocktail, but you're allergic to shellfish. And instead of chocolate lava cake, there's an oatmeal raisin cookie, and boy, do you hate oatmeal raisin cookies.

This is when I twist the knife.

I declare, "You must eat this food left-handed at exactly 3 in the afternoon. If you don't follow these instructions, you're living suboptimally, and therefore you don't care about your life or your health or your happiness or your family."

You'd probably toss me overboard faster than I could say "chocolate lava cake."

Why the hell would you suddenly base your value or worth on whether or not you could eat somebody else's plate of food? Even if that other somebody was really, really, ridiculously good-looking. Or a famous musician or influencer or celebrity.

There's a lot of money to be made by making us "less than" and then convincing us there is a "magic solution" to all our problems. We're told to buy something or eat a certain way or follow a certain protocol, because that's the key to success. They say, "I did it, and so can you!"

Maybe! But we now know better.

Over the coming years, as we're bombarded with advertisements and hype and optimized solutions, we can imagine we're standing in a cruise ship buffet line surrounded by others making their own plates:

Some people are focused on improving their health markers, which is why their plate has mostly protein, fruits, and vegetables on it.

Others are learning to enjoy food after years of toxic diet culture, which is why their plate includes a bowl of cereal and a cookie.

And others might be experiencing a gastrointestinal issue like celiac disease, which is why they are eating gluten-free options and saying no to cookies and dessert.

In all situations, we don't know what everybody else is going through. We haven't lived in their bodies. We don't have their goals or fears or dreams.

We need the confidence to put our own "food" on our own buffet plate, for our own reasons that fit our lifestyle, and not worry why others are eating the way they do.

We can certainly choose to *look* at other people's plates and say, "I'll try putting *some* of that on my plate," and then decide if we like it.

This is PACT in action:

We pause in the buffet line and process the options in front of us.

We accept that certain strategies or goals aren't right for us right now.

We change based on past experiences and future expectations.

We try it out.

Like a big experiment, we're trying to see if it's something that we enjoy, that helps us get results, and is something that we can keep doing. Once we've started, we can pay attention to the signals life gives us.

If it doesn't work for us, we can move on to the next thing without shame or guilt.

With each trip to the buffet line, we get a bit better at knowing what works for us, and which parts we can confidently ignore.

Key Insights

There's no one right way to do "the thing." Neal Stephenson needs four-hour blocks of uninterrupted time to write his sci-fi masterpieces. Agatha Christie wrote her books in fits and spurts, twenty to thirty minutes at a time, while living her life. Each of them found the path that worked for them. We can take solace in the fact that there many paths to reaching our goals.

Who wrote your rules? We all carry expectations based on how we were raised and what we learned from our parents, directly or indirectly. This is true for money, exercise, our relationship with food, careers, how we talk to one another, and more. Before we pick our next "thing," we should decide if the invisible scripts from our past are still serving us or need to be updated. Just because we've "always done it this way" doesn't mean we need to continue doing it that way.

Whose scorecard are you grading yourself on? We often compare ourselves to other people who are playing a different game from the one we are, comparing our day-to-day life with their highlight reels. Before blindly sending ourselves down *their* path thinking it'll solve our problems, we can decide what's important for *our* scorecard and our definition of success.

Ask "Is the juice worth the squeeze? Do I even like juice?" It's perfectly acceptable to admit we're not willing to put in the immense amount of work required to reach a certain goal. It's also okay to watch somebody else succeed at something we have no interest in. We get ourselves in trouble when we chase something we don't want, simply to impress people we don't like, doing something we're not actually interested in.

Build your own buffet plate. Every day, we're bombarded with people telling us about the one true way to get healthy or happy. Many of these strategies contradict one another. Think of these things like a cruise ship buffet plate. We get to build it based on what works for us, our goals, and our lifestyle, and we can confidently ignore the rest.

7

ESCAPE THE DOOM LOOP: HOW TO PROTECT YOURSELF FROM YOURSELF

Why "all-or-nothing" becomes "all, then nothing"

Confused bathroom patron: "What the hell are you doing?"

Fletcher Reed: "I'm kicking my ass, do you mind?"

—*Liar, Liar*

We've made our PACT, and we've even picked the next "thing" to try.

Now it's time to set our hopes sky-high, burn the boats, and go all in, right? And then we just do the thing. There's just one problem: We have a brain in our heads, and that brain is very good at self-sabotage when it comes to change. It's also great at critical self-judgment when we screw up, catastrophizing the smallest of mistakes, and derailing our progress just when things start to work.

In fact, our brains are so good at meddling that I dedicated this chapter to mental health and the complicated emotions that take place inside our heads.

After coaching tens of thousands of people at Nerd Fitness, we've identified the most common behavioral patterns and the most common cycles that busy humans tend to repeat over and over and over again when trying to make a change stick.

In fact, it's so common and sinister that I've given it a "movie villain" name:

The Doom Loop. (Cue the evil music!)

I'll first explain the loop (which will have you saying, "Crap, I do that."), and then I'll share specific "escape pods" that we can hop in when we find ourselves getting pulled back into this negative cycle.

What Is a Doom Loop?

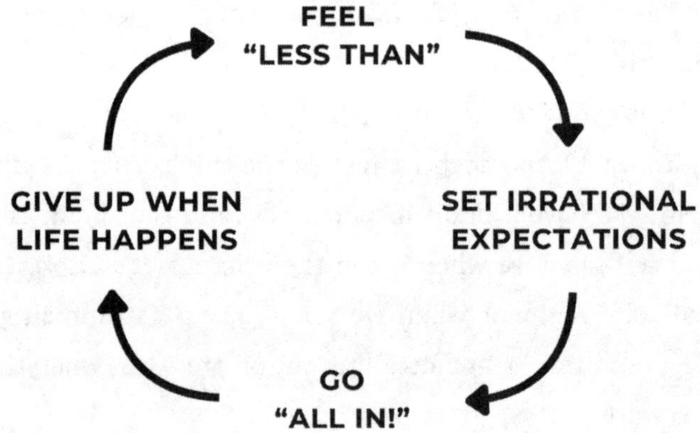

Step 1: We feel "less than." Our brains love to tell us that we're not enough. Not slim enough, not strong enough, not pro-

ductive enough, not happy enough, not rich enough. Even though we all know "comparison is the thief of joy," we can't help but pick some part of our life where we feel behind and compare it with somebody who's further ahead. We compare our "inside" to their exciting "outside."

We start each day feeling like lazy, lollygagging losers who are already behind and falling further behind.

Step 2: We set irrational expectations. But wait! We hear about "the one thing" that will solve all our problems. The optimized cold-plunge morning routine, the specific food or ingredient to avoid, the "one true workout," the perfect parenting routine for cherubic children. Surely this will make us happy.

It doesn't matter that we've *never* been able to follow a hyper-restrictive diet or wake up at 5 a.m. in the past. We tell ourselves, "But this time will be different."

Right now we're in the dreaming stage, and dreams are *fun.*

Author R. McCarthy James joked that all of her life plans require her to suddenly wake up with a "sense of discipline and adherence to a routine [she has] never once exhibited in [her] life."

We might be a dumpster fire today, but Future Us will be a Spartan god-king of self-discipline with the energy and ability to succeed.

We tell ourselves, "As long as things go according to plan, this will work and all my problems will be solved and unicorns will frolic and I'll have a great hair day!"

Step 3: We go all in! We make a GRAND DECLARATION! We buy the new journal. We download the strict meal plan. We spend $2,000 on fancy exercise equipment. We time-block our schedule in perfect thirty-minute increments. We set our alarm for 4:30 a.m.

We remember somebody once said, "How you do anything is how you do everything," so we set our expectation at perfect execution with militant dedication.

We decide anything worth doing is worth doing *perfectly, or not at all.*

We burn the boats.

We go all in.

And this works amazingly well . . . for, like, two weeks.

Step 4: "All-or-nothing" becomes "all, then nothing." Life happens. Work sucks or we get a flat tire or our kid gets sick or the dentist tells us we need a root canal. Something gets in the way, and our perfect streak is broken. That one missed day becomes a missed week, which becomes a missed month.

We get mad at ourselves for being undisciplined. We reinforce our insecurities and the belief that we're not enough until we succeed. Our brains tell us we failed because we *didn't try hard enough.*

And thus, we return to step 1 of the Doom Loop: Feeling "less than," except now with an extra sprinkle of guilt, frustration, and self-criticism.

And then we go around again.

We try more of the same things that haven't worked. We start our 5K training again even though we don't like running. We try yet another restrictive low-carb diet that we'll never stick with because carbs make life worth living. We set our alarm for 4:30 a.m. again even though we know we're just going to hit SNOOZE.

And we repeat this Doom Loop every few months, or every January, for years.

Fortunately, there's a better way. When our brain makes us feel "less than," when it starts to get critical that we're not doing enough, when it gets impatient and wants to race to the finish line, we can do things differently.

It's time to break free with some mental Escape Pods. They can help us interrupt the patterns that keep us struggling. They can give us a chance to reach escape velocity. And they can help us forgive ourselves when we inevitably screw up again.

Escape Pod #1: Let Our Thoughts Think Themselves

I have a liberating truth that can dramatically change our mental journey moving forward:

Thoughts think themselves.

I know it *feels* like our thoughts are ours. They're in our heads, which means we must *be* the creator of those thoughts, right?

But as neuroscientist Sam Harris writes in his book *Free Will*, "[We] are not the author of [our] thoughts. They simply arise, and [we] become aware of them." Our brains are giant satellite dishes, set to receive all the thoughts of the universe.

When we look at things this way, *of course* we can't control what thoughts we think. They just arrive all day, every day.[21]

We're kind of like Dan Aykroyd's character in *Ghostbusters*, who tried to clear his mind and instead thought about the Stay Puft Marshmallow Man. As Aykroyd explains to his fellow ghostbusters, "It just popped in there!"

See? Now you're thinking about the Stay Puft Marshmallow Man, a character you probably haven't thought about in ages.

This hopefully feels a bit liberating.

If we don't think our thoughts, then overly identifying with them or criticizing ourselves for having them doesn't make much sense. It would be like criticizing ourselves for having red hair or freckles.

Once we realize we're not our thoughts, we can then make the most freeing decision of all: to acknowledge our thoughts, and then turn the volume up on some, down on others, and let a few just fade away. We can be curious about the thoughts coming in, but we don't need to beat ourselves up for having them.

For those of us who have inner monologues[22] that are hypercritical, we can distance ourselves from our thoughts by giving that inner voice another name and personality.

---

21 Yes, the environment we're in, our mental health, how we were raised, our biochemistry, and more can factor into which thoughts enter our brain, even though we don't actively choose them.

22 If you don't have an inner monologue, meaning you don't have a conversation with yourself all day long, what's that like? It sounds peaceful.

Personally, I treat the thoughts in my head as if they're a random roommate I met through the internet.

His name is Chaz, and he has a ferret. Chaz means well, but he has no filter and just says whatever thought pops into his head. Chaz also struggles with negative self-talk and is full of anxiety, so I treat him with kindness like I would any friend going through a tough time.

At the same time, because I don't always agree with many of the thoughts Chaz yells out at random times, I don't mind turning down the volume on him from time to time. When Chaz comes in hot with a pile of negative thoughts and asks if I want some, I let him vent without judgment and then continue on with my day. I don't try to avoid these thoughts, drown them out, or cram them down. I invite them in, let them hang out without acting on them, and then watch as they eventually recede or disappear.

Regardless of what Chaz says, I actively decide to focus on what I believe is best for me, in my situation. I give myself the benefit of the doubt. I have kindness and grace for Chaz. I get curious as to where his thoughts might have come from and analyze these thoughts without internalizing them.

When I shared this idea of assigning a name to my thoughts with my audience, reader Elizabeth replied with the most delightful story:

> Once when I was in high school, I started chatting to myself in an Irish accent when I was walking home. (As an actor I often practice accents.) I found that I couldn't

say anything mean to myself when I was speaking in that accent. It was oddly nice. It felt like my kindest, wisest self had its own voice.

When we put some distance between our thoughts and ourselves, we can interrupt the pattern and decide whether or not they're worth listening to. When we can accept that our thoughts are simply things that happen without judging or embracing or identifying with them, we can pick and choose which ones are worth acting on.

Escape Pod #2: Forgive Ourselves for Being Human

I have another realization that might help when our hypercritical thoughts start to take over.

If tough love worked, it would have worked for us already.

We're not fighting Nazis in 1940s Europe here. We're not defending Earth from alien invaders. We're not performing open-heart surgery (at least not while reading this book). We're accountants and nurses and project managers and IT professionals and stay-at-home dads and supermoms working two jobs trying to get through a day without feeling miserable about ourselves. Sometimes, we are going to miss a workout and devour some ice cream and sleep in instead of going for our run.

This will happen because life will happen. We're going to

screw up a lot trying to implement all the stuff in this book. Life will happen to us, or around us, and some of it will be our fault. Our judgmental brain can't wait to assign blame and lash out at anybody and everybody (including ourselves).

It'll say, "I screwed up and I'm an asshat" or "I can't stick with this workout routine because I'm an asshat." Maybe it will blame everything on another person: "My boss is an asshat, and that's why I lashed out at my family today" or "My asshat kids are the reason I don't have time to work out!"

Hell, maybe we're just wildly gesticulating in every direction, screaming at the cosmos, "I'm surrounded by asshats!" Yes, I did use up all of my contractually allowable uses of the word "asshat," so you'll see more fun words from me moving forward.

Like "rapscallion."

For us to avoid getting trapped in the Doom Loop, my fellow rapscallion, we can pause and look at life honestly and clearly. Words have power, and when we are self-critical and leaning into "tough love," we set ourselves up for an emotional roller coaster, which is my least favorite kind of roller coaster.

Although our brain thinks it's helping by being critical, this behavior isn't serving us the way we think. In fact, research shows self-criticism is strongly related to depression and dissatisfaction. Fortunately, there's a much better strategy that creates better outcomes.

We can start by channeling the late poet Andrea Gibson, who wrote about resigning "from the position of My Own Worst Enemy," and firing our "inner critic, or at least demot[ing] it to part-time."

As for who should take the place of our critical voice, Kristin Neff, PhD, has some ideas.

She's a *New York Times* bestselling author and researcher whose work in behavioral psychology has impacted countless lives. She's a kind, caring, thoughtful, compassionate wife and mother as well.

And as she shares in her book *Self-Compassion,* she *also* had a challenging childhood.

Growing up with an absentee father, Neff spent most of her life looking for love and acceptance in all the wrong places. Like many overachievers, she was fueled by self-criticism, unrealistic expectations, and a negative inner voice. Although she had no problem extending kindness to others, she struggled to do the same for herself.

After her tumultuous marriage imploded, this voice grew louder than ever. After a year in India studying marriages for her dissertation, she returned to the University of California, Berkley, to complete her degree and pick up the pieces of her life.

Fortunately for her (and us!), this is when Neff discovered self-compassion at her weekly Buddhist meditation group.

She learned that being kind to herself didn't just mean putting a stop to self-judgment. It meant actively comforting herself the way she would comfort a friend in need.

She figured that if decades of being hypercritical of herself didn't work, maybe kindness would.

She doubled down on compassion research and discovered that after learning to be kind to herself, she could address the parts of her life that she had avoided dealing with for decades.

I figure if Kristin Neff can use self-compassion to quiet the critical voice in her head to create breakthroughs in her life, maybe we can do the same for ourselves. As she points out in *Self-Compassion*, we're worthy of kindness, no matter the cause of our struggle:

> Compassion is not only relevant to those who are blameless victims, but also those whose suffering stems from failures, personal weakness, or bad decisions. You know, the kind you and I make every day.

Life is hard enough. We don't need to make it harder by criticizing ourselves when things don't work out.

No matter what we're dealing with, we can start by remembering that we're part of an unbroken string of lovable goofballs who have struggled with similar things over the course of their lifetimes too. If you remember from our lessons on failure in chapter 1, our struggles connect us to our fellow humans: We're all trying, and there will be plenty of times when we don't do our best. That's okay.

We all know the Golden Rule: "Treat others the way you want to be treated."

The inverse is called the Silver Rule: "Don't treat others the way you wouldn't want to be treated."

We now have the Self-Compassion Rule: "Treat yourself the way you would treat a friend."

Think about how you respond when your friend is struggling, even if they were the one who screwed up. We know how to be kind and compassionate to them, because that's what friends do for each other, right? Good people have bad days too. We would never pile on to a friend that was hurting.

Maybe we can start doing the same for ourselves.

As Kristin Neff points out, "We can recognize that everyone has times when they blow it and treat ourselves kindly. Maybe we weren't able to put our best foot forward, but we tried, and falling flat on one's face is an inevitable part of life. An honorable part, in fact."

After my marriage ended, there was a day when I had to go pick up my belongings from the place I used to live.

As I was gathering my things and putting them into my car, I was really struggling with grief and sadness. My inner voice kept telling me, "I deserve to feel this way because things didn't work out."

Fortunately, I had been practicing self-compassion.

Rather than listening to that voice tell me, "Toughen up," I treated myself the way a friend would treat me and gave myself a pep talk:

> This is really hard, but I can do hard things. I've handled this situation the best I can, and I'm worthy of kindness.

I understand myself better because of what I've gone through. I have more compassion and empathy for others who are going through their own challenges. We're all trying to figure out life and find fulfillment and happiness. Our next attempt to change will hit roadblocks. A bunch of things will go wrong. When we misstep or life happens, it doesn't mean we need more tough love.

It means we need more kindness.

Escape Pod #3: Notice and Name to Regain Power

When we find ourselves falling back into the different steps of the Doom Loop, we can start to notice patterns in our behavior. If our brain tells us to feel "less than," if we get irrationally excited, or if we fall into "all-or-nothing" thinking, we can quickly apply a key tactic that can help us pause and break free.

In behavioral psychology, it's often referred to as "noticing and naming," where we literally name our feelings or thoughts as soon as we notice them.

It's an interruption that might just be enough for us to start reacting differently.

As my therapist constantly reminds me, awareness is the first step toward change.

Once we become aware of the triggers or patterns that cause us to fall back into the Doom Loop, we can actually do something about it.

We can start by practicing "thought labeling" or "affect labeling," common in mindfulness practices and therapies. It's when we acknowledge a thought, give it a name, and let it exist without judgment. By doing so, this puts some much needed separation from the thought and keeps us from letting that thought drive our behavior or send us spiraling further.

Words have power, so let's use them to pick us up, rather than drag us down. For example, we can remove "morality" where it doesn't belong. Eating a cookie isn't "bad" nor is it "cheating on" our diet. We can save what qualifies as "bad" for *actual* bad things like "robbed a blind nun," "tried to block the sun to then sell electricity back to the city of Springfield," and "didn't say 'bless you' when my dog sneezed."

Similarly, when our brain wants to sort everything into "ALL IN" or "OUT," we can remind ourselves of the truth:

There's very little in life that is "all-or-nothing." "Some" is a perfectly acceptable amount.

In psychologist Adam Mastroianni's essay, "So You Want to De-Bog Yourself," he shares his list of comical names for the ways his brain tries to sabotage him. For example, he often catches himself falling for the "waiting for jackpot" fallacy: His brain tells him to wait around for a solution that has *only* upsides, *no* downsides, and solves all his problems, instead of trying the best option right now. Not surprisingly, that solution never seems to come.

He names his thoughts to avoid the most insidious lie his brain tells constantly: that he's "stuck in a situation unlike any [he], or anyone else, has ever seen before."

Personally, I've had a lot of practice labeling my thoughts while writing this book. I've battled anxiety around perfectionism and potential outcomes I have no control over. I literally say to myself out loud, "I feel anxiety in my stomach. I can't control the outcome. I am only going to focus on what I can control."

It's actually pretty amazing how we can affect our behavior through changing the words we use and how we interpret our thoughts and emotions.

Escape Pod #4: Understand What Scares You and Lean In

In the film adaptation of *The Fellowship of the Ring,* Frodo Baggins meets the mysterious Aragorn at the Inn of the Prancing Pony. Aragorn asks Frodo if he is frightened by the evil wraiths that are chasing him. When Frodo meekly replies, "Yes," Aragorn retorts, "Not nearly frightened enough. I know what hunts you."

We might not be in Middle-earth, but our coaches at Nerd Fitness know this all too well, so we ask every coaching client:

> You're excited now, but what are you scared will happen a month from now?

Maybe the client is afraid they'll fall back into "all-or-nothing" thinking, or that a work project will cause them to cope emotionally with unhealthy foods. Asking this question gives the coach a chance to start planning for chaos and those inevitable problems *before they happen.*

If we know we're going to get impatient or bored or life will get chaotic in a few weeks, great! If we know our schedule is set while the kids are in school but will go off the rails once summer vacation starts, even better. We can now prepare for these things.

In business terms, it's often called a "premortem": Before a project has started, everybody gets a chance to share why they think the project could fail. The goal is to literally identify all the things that might go wrong or why it won't be successful. They can then get to work on setting up contingency plans for those inevitable problems.

We can do the same thing with whatever experiment we're attempting next:

"I'll get stuck at work and have to order fast food."

"My kid will get sick at daycare in the next few weeks, and I'll miss a workout."

"I'll drink too much alcohol when I get socially anxious at the holiday party."

Over a long enough timeline, potential problems become inevitable ones.

We won't be able to predict everything that could go wrong, but we can prepare for *something* to go wrong and protect against making things worse.

Instead of having a better plan, we can focus instead on preparing for whatever plan we have to fall apart.

If we normally go to the gym after work and it's always busy, we can assume that some of the equipment will be in use. By already knowing one or two *other* exercises that work the same muscle groups, we can simply do those instead of getting frustrating and waiting around.

If we normally let our nutrition go off the rails while traveling, we can identify a few solid options at some specific restaurants near our work hotel before the trip starts. Suddenly, we're not stuck *only* eating fast food and then feeling bad the next day.

There's another benefit of expecting our fears to happen: A premortem gives us a chance to switch from defense (reacting to problems) to offense (anticipating problems and coming up with potential solutions).

Best of all, when the inevitable happens and something goes wrong, we won't be surprised. We already expected it!

By taking the time to think through what could go wrong and having a simple backup plan, when emotions are high and everything is on fire, we have already done the work. We won't fall back into "all-or-nothing" thinking, over-catastrophizing small problems, or criticizing ourselves for not being perfect.

(Not that any of us do this.)

Escape Pod #5: Overcome Impatience with Healthier Expectations

I'm in the process of building a meditation habit for the eight-hundred-twenty-seventh time. These quotes from Jon Kabat-Zinn's book *Wherever You Go, There You Are* gave me some much needed perspective:

> For most of us, it takes years and depends a good deal on your motivation and the intensity of your practice.
>
> So, at the beginning, you might want to stay with the breath, or use it as an anchor to bring you back when you are carried away.
>
> Try it for a few years and see what happens.

That final sentence, "Try it for a few years and see what happens," completely shifted my expectation and timeline for building a habit of meditating. In the past, I would think, "If I could just meditate for thirty days straight, then I'll be good at mindfulness. Maybe then I'll finally have peace!"

I was trying to "win." I couldn't wait until I got "there." I was going about this all wrong. My goal should have been to sit with my thoughts and focus on my breath, and try to do that on more days than not. That's it. I needed to focus on the process, not the end goal.

We're all in such a rush to reach the finish line for whatever goal or habit we're trying to accomplish. We think it should take a certain number of weeks or months to write an essay or book. We decide we should lose X pounds in Y weeks, or that it should take Z days before we're effortlessly following our exercise routine. In all scenarios, our timeline is always based on things going "according to plan. . . ."

Unfortunately, there's this thing called Hofstadter's Law, coined by Douglas Hofstadter. It dictates that no matter what we're doing, it will always take longer than we expect, even when we take into account Hofstadter's Law.

Instead of setting "irrational expectations" on how fast we should reach a goal, only to get frustrated when our timeline is off, we can choose to do things differently. If we expect everything will take longer than we want, we might pick more reasonable goals, sustainable routines, and enjoyable activities that we don't mind doing for a longer period of time. Paradoxically, this often results in more progress faster, because we stop jumping from quick fix to quick fix (and never getting any traction), and we stop going all in and then giving up.

When I find myself getting impatient about racing to a finish line, I try to ask myself the opposite question: "What's the least amount of change I can follow through with consistently, to be able to reach my goal eventually?"

After all, most of our experiments, like exercising or making healthier food choices, are things we are trying to do for the rest of our lives, so we might as well find a way to enjoy them.

Once we accept everything takes longer than expected, we can then just focus on doing "the thing" today and let momentum do its job.

Pause, Accept, Change, and Try a New Thought

Learning to work with (instead of against) our brains will be a lifelong adventure, but hopefully this whets your appetite and has you interested in getting to know what's going on between your ears on a deeper level. Whether it's therapy with a mental health professional, learning to meditate, or practicing mindfulness, prioritizing our mental health is never a bad idea.

Personally, learning to be kinder to myself has been the most challenging and important thing I've done for myself over the past few years. I've learned to sit with my uncomfortable thoughts. I've worked hard to spend less time ruminating on the past and anxiously worrying about the future. Instead, I try to "be here now" as often as I can, to quote the mindfulness teacher Ram Dass. I don't always succeed, but I do my best and keep working on it.

We're going to have negative, critical thoughts pop into our heads. They will try to make us feel less than and not enough. Although our brains think they're helping protect us from other people's criticisms by criticizing ourselves first, the result ends up being a continued spiral of shame and self-loathing. When these thoughts arrive, we can decide which ones deserve our attention, and which ones can be acknowledged and then turned down.

It's amazing what we can do if we start to identify all the ways our brain tries to pull us back into the Doom Loop.

We can pause long enough to realize we aren't our thoughts.

We can accept the thought and label it, and then change how much power we allow it to have over us.

We can then try to do things differently moving forward.

Key Insights

Beware the Doom Loop, where "all-or-nothing" becomes "all, then nothing." The Doom Loop starts with us feeling "less than." We then get irrationally excited that "the next thing" will solve all our problems. And then we go "all in!" with a new journal or calendar or restrictive diet for two weeks, and then give up when life gets in the way. Once we see these patterns, we can start to see them playing out in our lives repeatedly and get to work on getting out of the Loop.

Remember that thoughts think themselves. Life is complicated, we humans are bizarre, and we are not our thoughts. Our brains are satellite dishes that receive thoughts, and we get to choose which ones we turn up and which ones we turn down. By setting aside judgment, we can stop beating ourselves up when these thoughts arrive after a mistake. We can also give a name or personality or accent to our thoughts to put some distance between ourselves and them, which can help us separate our identity and give us a chance to react differently this time.

Forgive yourself. We often make things worse by criticizing and berating ourselves when something goes wrong. If tough love worked, it would have worked already. Instead, self-compassion is a proven strategy to start seeing life clearly for what it is. We can embrace the self-compassion rule: We can treat ourselves the way we treat our friends. Even when we make a mistake or don't show up as our best selves, we're still worthy of kindness.

Notice and name your thoughts to take away their power. Our brains are weird, and our thoughts are even stranger. To interrupt our thought patterns, we can notice them and give them fun names. This helps take away their power and reminds us that we don't have to be captured by our thoughts or beholden to the same behavior patterns forever. We can acknowledge them, recognize the pattern, and then do things differently moving forward.

Lean in to your fears and conduct a premortem. Before we start our next experiment, we can do a premortem and identify the things that could go wrong and prepare for how we'll solve those problems. We know that on a long enough timeline, any potential problem becomes an inevitable one. We can have alternative workouts, emergency meals in the freezer, and contingency plans for when life happens. This reminds us that there are many steps between "all" and "nothing," and that "some" is a perfectly acceptable amount.

Remind ourselves that change takes time. Hofstadter's Law says everything will always take longer than we expect, even when we take into account Hofstadter's Law. We shouldn't be surprised when the project or experiment or habit or routine takes longer than we want. Paradoxically, picking smaller goals with a more reasonable timeline often results in faster progress, because we stop jumping from one quick fix to the next and instead stick with an experiment long enough to see progress and build momentum.

8

HOW TO KEEP DOING THE THING

Ten Strategies that Will (Probably) Work

We do not do this because it is easy. We do it because we thought it would be easy.

—Internet meme

This chapter is written specifically for you.

Yes, you.

I wrote this to help protect against that *exact* moment, three to four weeks from now, when we're at our most vulnerable. When we're on the verge of sliding back into old patterns and destructive behaviors, and slipping back into the "all-or-nothing" mentality in the Doom Loop.

That moment when motivation wears thin, and willpower is low. When we hear the siren song of "Things are busy now, so I'll try again later when things get less busy." We've done that too many times before.

So rather than hoping it doesn't happen *again*, let's do some work *now*, while we're motivated and excited, to protect Future Us from that pitfall!

For us to build a long-term sustainable relationship with change, we need to be fairly consistent, most of the time, and restart quickly when we miss a day. Simple, but not easy.

Which is why we're going to build "self-efficacy," a term coined by psychologist Albert Bandura. It sounds fancy, but it just means belief in our ability to make positive change in our lives.

There are four components to Bandura's self-efficacy:

- "mastery experiences," when we personally complete a task or goal
- "vicarious experiences," when we see somebody else succeed at a task or goal
- "verbal persuasion," when we get encouragement and support
- "physiological and affective states," how we *feel,* our mood that day, etc.

I've done my best throughout this book to help you build belief that you're capable of change (#3). I also hope I've given you a bit of guidance on how to navigate your emotions (#4), so the strategies below are focused mostly on #1 and #2.

These are also the strategies we've used most effectively to help people in the Nerd Fitness community (the Rebellion) build better habits and make change that sticks after years or decades of feeling stuck.

Now, this is a BIG chapter, so I don't mind if you skim these ten strategies like you're browsing a buffet to see which one grabs your attention. The goal is to provide ourselves with definitive proof that says "I am capable of doing this."

I don't know if you're going to pick a 5K or write a book or start a new hobby with your children, but I'm excited for you. Mostly because I'm easily excitable, but also because I believe you can do this.[23]

Strategy #1: Get a Quick Win Doing the Thing

Whenever we start working with new clients, we try to get them a quick, meaningful win right away to create momentum in the right direction. We're looking for something that signals, "Maybe this time *will* be different!" For some, that might mean completing their first workout, or for others it's filling out their first page in a journal or making their first sustainable dietary change.

This sends a signal to the part of our brains that's worried about falling back into the well-worn grooves of the Doom Loop. We can't get different results if we don't do things differently, right?

So let's start by doing literally *anything differently.*

If you've ever seen the movie *Garden State*, Natalie Portman's precocious character, Samantha, is tired of feeling unoriginal and stuck in suburban hell. So she makes a very deliberate, strange choice:

> You know what I do when I feel completely unoriginal?

23 Yes, this component #3 from self-efficacy in action!

> I make a noise, or I do something that no one has ever done before, and then I can feel unique, even if it's only for, like, a second.

She then flails her arms and makes a weird noise. Although I don't think this is a full workout, the idea of doing something new certainly has merit. We want to signal to our skeptical thoughts that this next attempt might be different, which can only be true if we do something different.

Next, we want an early "win," like when the owner at the local sandwich shop punches the first two holes into our "buy nine subs, get one free" card. They want us to feel invested, because it gives us momentum and makes us want to come back. It tricks our brain into thinking we don't nearly have as far to go to "reach our goal" as we thought.

Yes, this is a psychological trick. Who cares!

We're trying to give ourselves the best chance to start differently. Most of life is trying to negotiate with our brains anyway, hoping they will get out of the way long enough to let us *do the thing* more often than not.

Feel free to put "Create a to-do list" at the top of your to-do list and then cross it off. Make your bed in the morning and get yourself a "win" before you've even had your coffee. Hell, feel free to do something right now that's different from what Past You would have done.

No, seriously, right now.

Do five push-ups on the side of your desk or against the wall.

Pick up your kid and do a squat.

Go for a two-minute walk.

Is this enough to create a change? Of course not! But it's a start, and a signal to ourselves that we've begun.

Action creates motivation, which encourages us to take more action.

I have to remind myself of this truth constantly. When I'm stressed and overwhelmed and grappling with a problem, my brain tells me I don't have time for a ten-minute walk.

Of course, if I can get myself out of the house, five minutes into my walk, I *always* feel better and more energized, my problems don't seem as overwhelming, and a solution often presents itself.

When I don't have time for a ten-minute walk, I probably need a twenty-minute walk.

My brain also *loves* to tell me, "I'm too stressed and anxious to meditate," even though I know meditation is exactly what would help with my stress and anxiety.

Sigh. Brains are fun.

Strategy #2: Make the Thing Fun

We're led to believe that doing the thing must be hard.

We need to rise and grind. If we're not a dripping puddle of sweat on the ground after the workout, then we weren't working hard enough. We must push through pain and be disciplined and eat glass and overcome weakness to succeed.

Maybe! Yes, there's value in doing hard things, and it can be rewarding to push through resistance and overcome hardship.

But if we find ourselves often giving up when faced with a grueling routine that we don't enjoy, which we started because we hoped it would solve all our problems, maybe there's another way.

I feel for people who finally work up the courage to exercise, only to attend a class or activity they end up hating. They leave that class thinking, "If *that's* what it takes to be healthy, I'm out. I'd rather stay unhealthy." They just picked the wrong type of exercise for them.

I own a fitness company, and you couldn't pay me to run a marathon or go to a boot-camp class. I don't enjoy them. But I DO love picking up weights and doing handstands and playing golf and going for long walks, so *that's how I exercise*! I have fun and stay fit.

If we're just trying to be healthier and get ourselves to move more, *any* movement counts.

We can try out different kinds of exercise until we find one that fits our personality, schedule, and lifestyle. It might be swing dance classes, or joining a running club that's more about the conversation than the run. Maybe it's playing *Beat Saber* with our virtual reality headset, going for a hike, strength training, or Live Action Role Playing (LARPing).

There's always a way to add some humor and fun to more serious tasks too.

At Nerd Fitness, we love to come up with fun names for everybody's workout program. "Mike's Workout A" is boring. But "Mike's workout plan to fight Thanos" suddenly has some brightness and energy to it. I once spent a year turning my life into a video game by assigning point totals to life quests and challenges. I called it my *Epic Quest of Awesome.*

Now, not every part of life gives us a chance to "pick the fun option," and sometimes we have to do boring and un-fun tasks. Author Gregory McKeown encourages us to still ask the question "What if this *could* be fun?"

The most common strategy here is "temptation bundling": We combine the necessary task with a fun task and do both at the same time.

We can clean the house while blasting our favorite songs or walk on the treadmill while watching our favorite reality TV show.

Maybe we're scared to try yoga, but going to a puppy yoga class with our best friend makes it more fun. In his book *Effortless*, McKeown shares the story of how he was dreading a series of phone calls he needed to make. So he decided to make himself a fun cocktail and make those calls from a hot tub.

Here's my personal example that has surprisingly helped a *lot* of people improve their dental hygiene.

After decades of neglect, I finally built the habit of flossing.

How? By putting my floss in the shower.

When I'm standing under a delightfully hot shower (I'm out on the whole "cold showers make you more alpha" trend) and singing a song off-key and feeling pretty happy, that's when I floss my teeth. Yep, it's weird. But it works for me, and surprisingly for multiple friends who all told me they now keep their floss in the shower too. Let's not be afraid to get creative!

Strategy #3: Make the Thing Beneficial

Right now we're motivated. But three weeks from now, life is going to get in the way, and motivation will abandon us when we need it most. Which is why we can spend a bit of time *now* coming up with a damn good reason *why* we're trying to change.

There are many parts of life that are on the other side of doing hard things. When we can get ourselves to do something that sucks in the moment but is beneficial after the fact, amazing things can happen.

As personal trainer Andrew Coates says, "Every day you hit the gym when you don't *feel* like it buys you a day off when you really *need* it." This doesn't just apply to going to the gym either, but for anything challenging worth doing.

The more we can remind ourselves that it feels good to *have done* hard things, particularly on days when we don't feel like it, the better chance we have at sustainable progress. It can help teach us that we're capable of following through even when our brains want us to say no.

Having a deeper motivation behind our actions can help us not give up when things get tough.

Getting up early to go for a run in the dark sucks, but we know we'll feel great after the fact, along with a sense of pride that we're committing to our goals.

Eating a healthy salad is less enjoyable in the moment than fast food, but we know we'll feel better after the fact and proud that we made a choice in line with our longer-term goals.

At Nerd Fitness, we call this our "Big Why."

If we can attach a deeper purpose or more personal reason behind why we're trying to change something in our lives, it can help get us through that lull a few weeks from now.

Maybe we're using twenty seconds of courage to attend a weekly improv class to build social skills so that we can start dating again.

Maybe we're lifting weights to be an inspiration to our daughter and show her that moms can be strong too.

Personally, I started exercising to build confidence and feel better about myself. Pretty soon, I realized I was getting motivated lifting heavier weights each time. Going to the gym was no longer a means to an end, but something I looked forward to.

Strength training had become part of my identity, and the gym had become my happy place, something I never would have expected when starting out.

If we can attach a "Big Why" to our activity, we're more likely to follow through with it, even when that motivation starts to wane a few weeks later.

Strategy #4: Make the Thing Necessary

Do you know the tale of the Sirens in Homer's *Odyssey*?

The main character, Odysseus in the Greek version or Ulysses in the Latin version, is preparing to sail his crew past a dangerous island of Sirens who sing beautiful music. This music is so alluring that anybody who hears it loses all control and will sail toward the island, crashing their boat on the rocks.

Luckily, Ulysses receives life-saving advice that changes everything. In *Circe*, Madeline Miller's retelling of this ancient tale, the misunderstood goddess explains how the captain can save his crew:

> [For] the Sirens, there you may use your tricks. Fill your men's ears with wax, and leave your own free. If you tie yourself to the mast, you may be the first man to ever hear their song and tell the tale.

This allows "current Ulysses" to protect "future Ulysses." By having his men tie him to the mast and NEVER untie him under any circumstances, he removes his own willpower as a necessary element for success. Meanwhile, his men (with plugged ears) could row safely without temptation past the island. As author Cory Doctorow points out in his essay on Ulysses Pacts:

> Ulysses was strong enough to know that he would someday be weak. He expressed his strength by guarding against his weakness. . . . [A "Ulysses pact" is made] when you take some possibility off the table during a mo-

> ment of strength in recognition of some coming moment of weakness.

Instead of hoping we can find enough willpower to stay on track, we can reduce our need to use it.

I used a plethora of Ulysses Pacts to get this book done. I use a program on my Mac to block every fun website on my computer between the hours of 5 a.m. and 8 p.m. I have a program on my phone that blocks every fun app during that same time period.

When my brain is hearing the siren song of YouTube, and I'm desperate to avoid the uncomfortable reality of my book needing to be edited, I am physically unable to seek out that distraction.

I then tell myself, "Welp, I might as well just finish my book and then feel better about life, sigh."

(By the way, it did feel great turning this in.)

We're not just limited to protecting against weaknesses. We can also encourage positive behavior through adjusting our environment:

Let's say we're trying to get more exercise. We can do things like parking at the end of the parking lot to get extra steps in, opting for "walk and talk" meetings instead of sitting in a conference room, or choosing to walk instead of riding in a golf cart while playing nine holes after work.

Okay, there's one more diabolical strategy to get us to stay on target, and it almost always works. To overcome future moments when motivation and willpower are low, we can set up a situation in which the negative consequences for *not doing* the thing are so massive that we actually just follow through on our goals.

And what's the most effective motivator? Money.

My friend and author Nir Eyal made a financial commitment to another friend that he would have a draft of his next book done by Christmas or he would pay his friend $10,000. Whenever Nir felt the pull of "I don't want to do this thing," the very real fear of losing $10,000 was enough to get him to just do the damn thing. Comically, this was how he finished the draft for his now-bestselling book on sticking to one's goals, *Indistractable*.

Strategy #5: Reduce the Distance Between You and the Thing

Actor Terry Crews was asked on a Reddit "Ask Me Anything" how to build the routine of going to the gym, and he recommended an unusual strategy.

> Go to the gym, and just sit there, and read a magazine, and then go home. And do this every day. Go to the gym, don't even work out. Just GO.
>
> Because the habit of going to the gym is more important than the workout. Because it doesn't matter what you do. You can have fun—but as long as you're having fun, you continue to do it.

Now, we know that sitting in the gym lobby won't make us magically fit.

But remember that "going to the gym" is dozens of steps and decisions. So even if we only make it as far as the front lobby, that still counts as progress! We've already figured out how to sign up for the membership, where to park, how to get there, and more. All we have left is the final step: exercise.

It all comes down to proximity.

The closer we are to the thing, the more likely we are to do the thing.

In Terry Crews's example, we might see somebody from work who is an experienced weight lifter. Maybe we'll decide one day to work up the courage to step on that treadmill, or go pick up a dumbbell, or sign up for a class that looks fun. The opportunity for serendipity can happen because we were in the right place at the right time. If we bring ourselves closer to the action or activity, it increases the likelihood that we do the thing more often.

Let's decrease the proximity:

Carrying a book around with us makes us more likely to read instead of scrolling on our phones.

If we want to try stand-up comedy, hanging out at open mics gets us much closer to eventually getting on stage.

Joining a dance class or singles night makes the distance between us and meeting new single people much shorter than sitting at home on the couch.

Putting a pull-up bar in our office doorframe makes us more likely to hang or do a pull-up every time we walk under it.

The shorter the distance between us and the thing, the more opportunities we have to take action, the more likely we'll be to actually do the thing.

You might have already figured this out, but the opposite also works for trying to do *less* of a particular thing too. Removing certain foods from the house, putting the PlayStation or Nintendo in the closet, deleting certain smartphone apps, and so on. Adding distance between us and the activity makes us *less* likely to do it. Combine this with a Ulysses Pact, and we're now using our laziness as a strength.

Strategy #6: Find People Who Already Do the Thing

In Larry McMurtry's *Lonesome Dove,* former Texas Ranger Augustus McCrae has a cattle ranch that he operates with a colorful cast of characters. At one point, McCrae added the phrase "Uva uvam vivendo varia fit" to the Hat Creek Cattle Company sign, because it "seemed to him a beautiful motto, whatever it meant." (McCrae decided Latin "was mostly for looks anyway.")

Although McCrae might not have known what the phrase meant, the rest of us can decipher it (thanks, internet!). Some of the phrasing is an incorrect translation of Latin, but I think we can forgive a cowboy back in 1870 for such a mistake.

Let's look at the phrase, roughly translated: "A grape changes color when it sees another grape."

In other words, we are heavily influenced by the people we spend the most time with. Over time, we start to become more like the people around us (which can be good or bad!).

If there's a particular goal we're trying to accomplish, or a behavior we're looking to change, we can choose to spend more time with certain people (and less time with others).

When I started Nerd Fitness, I was just a twentysomething dude with minimal responsibilities, and my audience was (and still is) far more diverse: single moms, night-shift nurses, overworked lawyers, janitors, and people from all walks of life.

But things really took off when the community started helping each other out: They could learn from other people like them, who were in the same stage of life and facing similar struggles. This can apply to so many parts of life.

Rather than learning from an unrelatable influencer or celebrity, we're better off sitting down for coffee with our friend from our church or men's group or online community who also has kids and asking them how they did it. If we've seen them succeed in a way we believe we're capable of succeeding, it can give us some encouragement that maybe we can change too.

This is that second component of Bandera's self-efficacy called "vicarious experiences of social models." Observing other relatable people who have succeeded makes us more likely to believe we can change too.

As James Clear discusses in *Atomic Habits*,[24] we should try to spend more time with people whose default behavior is our

---

24 I know quoting James in a behavior change book is cliché at this point, but he featured Nerd Fitness is his wonderful book, so I think it's okay.

desired behavior. Find people who do the thing regularly and we'll be more likely to also do it regularly. Clear explains:

> Your culture sets your expectation for what is "normal." Surround yourself with people who have the habits you want to have yourself. You'll rise together.

As the saying goes, if we want to go fast, go alone; if we want to go far, go together:

- Want to become a runner? Join a running club (or start one).
- Want to become more social? Spend time with your outgoing friends.
- Want to become a better writer? Start a group chat with other writers and share your work.

Strategy #7: Protect the Thing with Boundaries

The 2022 Danish film *Speak No Evil*[25] is a horror movie that asks the question, "How much are you willing to compromise your boundaries and values to avoid uncomfortable conversations?"

As a conflict-avoidant people pleaser, it's one of the scariest films I've ever seen.

It made me dive deeper into my own boundaries and self-

25 The 2024 English remake isn't as bleak, but it's still very uncomfortable.

respect, and get curious about why I often put everybody else's feelings ahead of my own. I will bend over backward to keep the peace. I'll do whatever I can to not offend. I'll overcommit. I'll put myself in really frustrating situations, simply because I don't want to disappoint others.

Long story short, I would NOT have done well in *Speak No Evil.*

I used to think my people-pleasing was me being nice. Only after burning out repeatedly did I realize I was too focused on everybody else to have my own needs addressed too. I was being disrespectful to myself.

Don't be like Past Steve.

Healthy boundaries can be life-changing, because they allow us to actually consider our needs too.

Being able to say no might feel bad in the moment, especially if we're used to always saying yes. The truth is that these boundaries are a sign of self-respect. Boundaries show us that that our time is valuable and that we are worth protecting too.

We have to put on our own oxygen mask before we help others with theirs. We must have the time and energy to take care of ourselves first so that we can show up as our best selves for the important people in our lives. That means standing up for ourselves and protecting our time to do the things that we need to do.

I know there are a lot of amazing overworked parents reading this book who haven't considered their own needs in a long time, which is completely understandable. But hear me out.

As Dr. Pooja Lakshmin points out in her book, *Real Self-Care*, establishing boundaries can be the ultimate form of self-care if we're able to ask for what we need:

> . . . You must be willing to make yourself vulnerable—whether that means having uncomfortable conversations to set boundaries or making the clear and deliberate choice to prioritize one aspect of your life over another.

We can develop the ability to say, "This is important to me, and I need the space to do it." It might mean finding the courage to: 1) stop overcomitting 2) ask our spouse for help and 3) tell our children to finally stop overcommitting, asking our spouse for help, and tell our children we need some alone time too.

I know this is tough, particularly when it means we might disappoint others who, knowingly or not, are used to relying on our overgenerosity.

Fortunately, we'll encounter *plenty* of opportunities to establish and to reinforce our boundaries:

Maybe we have a family member who comments on our food choices while out at a restaurant. After a few years, we've finally decided this behavior is no longer welcome.

Maybe our kids and our spouse are used to us managing the entire house and doing *everything*. It's now time to have a conversation with them about how they can start helping.

Maybe we have a boss that continually emails us on nights and weekends and wants instant answers without ever considering our workload or the fact that we have young kids.

Congratulations! We have officially identified some areas of our life in which boundaries could help clear more space for us.

Because everybody lives different lives, some people might not be aware that their behavior is impacting us. It's our responsibility to establish our boundaries and let others know when those boundaries are crossed. We can be kind, as long as we remember their emotions aren't our responsibility to manage.

Outside of just clearly stating our boundaries, we can also explain our boundaries with rules. In *Clear Thinking*, author Shane Parrish points out:

> In a quirk of psychology, people typically don't argue with your personal rules. They just accept them as personal features of who you are. People question decisions, but they respect rules.

To cut down on the "just live a little" responses, we can share our "no alcohol on weekdays" or "no junk food at work" rule.

To help protect against pushy salespeople, we can explain that we have a "never make decisions over the phone" rule.

When we establish healthy boundaries and put reasonable rules in place, we can remove the guilt we might feel around needing to manage everybody else's emotions and finally have our own needs met.

Strategy #8: Half-Ass the Thing

Let's decide we're not going to let "busy" be the reason we stop. Instead, we're going to constantly redefine what "done" means for us.

We're going to stop asking, "Do I have time to do the thing?"

Instead we're going to ask, "How much of the thing do I have time for?"

There's no hard-and-fast rule that says, "I have to do it for X minutes or the world explodes." We picked a random thing to try. That's it.

Instead of looking at the thing like an on/off switch, we can look at it like a dial that can be adjusted up or down.[26]

When our schedule allows, we can turn the dial all the way up to 10 (or 11, if you're a *Spinal Tap* fan) and do our full workout. On days when things are a bit busy, we can turn the dial down to a 5 or 6. And on days when life is completely crazy, we can turn it all the way down to a 1.

As long as we don't turn it off, it's a win.

Because exercise is the most common example, let's go there.

Some people *love* building "streaks" and find them motivating. For example, investor Todd Simkin explained to host Shane Parrish on *The Knowledge Project* podcast how doing something every day is easier for him than doing it occasionally. This removes the bargaining tactics his brain might try to use to not follow through:

> I find it easy to exercise seven days a week. I found it really hard to exercise five days a week. The reason was because

26 Hat tip to Precision Nutrition, where I first heard this analogy!

every morning the alarm goes off at 5 a.m., it's really easy to not have your feet hit the ground and get going.

It's really easy to say, "Well, I need to take two days off anyway. This can be one of the days that I take off."

If we're trying to build a streak of exercising, we can adjust our definition of "exercise" each day to keep the streak alive. Depending on what our schedule looks like, we can have a backup plan ready to execute at a moment's notice:

Dial at 10: I go to the gym and do my sixty-minute strength workout and crush it!

Dial at 6: I have only thirty minutes before soccer practice, so I'll do the first three exercises and skip the last three.

Rather than thinking 6 is a step *down* from 10, it's a different setting on the dial based on what life throws at us. That's it.

In both situations, the end result is "I did something!"

What if we don't have enough time to go to the gym at all? We can adjust our definition of "workout" down to the lowest possible action.

Dial at 1: I did five squats while holding my newborn baby in her bedroom before the rest of the house woke up. Workout complete. Streak intact.

When building a streak, action counts. As long as it's not 0, mission accomplished. It's not better or worse, just different.

Strategy #9: Skipped the Thing Today? Do It Tomorrow.

Want to know the fastest and simplest way to *not* let "all or nothing" become "all, then nothing?" By embracing a tactic that sounds *so simple* it couldn't possibly work, and yet it does.

Let's say you normally shower each morning before work. Unfortunately, today is the day that life gets in the way. Your kid ate too much Lucky Charms and threw up all over the floor, and now the dog is eating it. You scramble to get him ready in time to catch the school bus, but he misses it. You throw on some deodorant, splash some water on your face, and drop him off at school before heading to the office.

Technically, you have failed at showering today.

How do you respond when this happens? Do you say, "I suck. I have no discipline. I'm a loser. I didn't plan well enough. I'll try showering again next month."

Of course not! That would be absurd.

If you don't shower today for any reason, it has zero reflection on who you are as a person.

It doesn't mean you need to change your whole shower strategy and buy another book about how to shower like a champion. You don't need to find a new podcast on the showering habits of successful people. No grand shower declarations. No shower shame or guilt.

Today was a tough day, and that's it. You move on with your life and shower tomorrow. This is how we're going to make imperfect progress for the rest of life: by being pretty consistent, most of the time.

Many years ago, I meditated every day for six months straight using a meditation app. I made sure I didn't miss a single day so that I could earn a little digital badge of a brain with flexing arms for my six-month achievement.

I was so good at meditating . . . until I wasn't.

I missed one day due to circumstances outside my control.

No big deal, right? I mean, 180 out of 181 days is *almost* perfect. In the grand scheme of things, that's a 99.4 percent success rate. Except it isn't 100 percent, which is what my brain focused on. My streak had ended, and the app now said ZERO-DAY STREAK.

Because my expectation was "perfection without compromise," I failed. And not only that, but for me to reach a new personal best, I would need to be perfect for the next 181 days. That felt so daunting that I just quit meditating altogether.

It took me *years* before I tried meditating again, when I finally accepted reality. I had let the meditation streak become more important than why I had started in the first place: to sit quietly with my breath more days than not.

This applies to whatever skill experiment we're working on:

When life gets in the way today, "shower tomorrow" and move on.

When we skip a workout because we got a flat tire, do the workout tomorrow and move on.

If we have a travel day of eating fast food, follow it up with a healthy breakfast tomorrow and move on.

If we forget to journal or have a bad day because work sucked, say, "Okay, let's try again tomorrow."

I know, I know. This sounds so simple. Simple, but not easy.

In my experience, how somebody responds to a missed day is probably the greatest predictor of success or failure I've seen over seventeen years of helping people build healthier habits. If they "shower tomorrow" and check in, they've got a damn good chance of succeeding. If they stick their head in the sand or ghost us because they're full of self-loathing, guilt, or shame, their road to success will be much harder until they can build this skill.

Strategy #10: Stack Wins Every Time We Do the Thing

So many of our daily decisions are a fifty-fifty coin flip:

To go for a run or watch *one more* episode of *The Office*.

To work on our book or scroll social media.

To finally cook dinner or to hit a button on our phone and order takeout.

I'm not passing judgment on *either side* of the above, as there's a time and place for both. I'm simply pointing out how much of our life is dictated by a series of small decisions that happen all day, every day.

If we make the same old decision nine times out of ten . . . that still leaves the tenth time when we do something differently. It counts! And every "win" helps us increase the belief in ourselves that this time will be different. After all, every long-term change had to begin with a single different decision.

The one time we cook at home instead of opting to buy fast food.

The one time we went to the yoga class instead of going to the bar.

The one time we said yes to socializing with our new coworkers instead of staying home.

Once we *start* getting some wins, our only goal should be to *keep* adding wins to the pile. This gives us tangible evidence of how much we've already done. As they say, we're aiming for progress over perfection, which means we just want to keep stacking wins.

This can be done by keeping tally marks for every time we complete a workout, keeping track of how many total miles we've biked, or even creating a fun system that shows us visually how much we've accomplished.

The most popular technique associated with this includes a glass jar and lots of items or tokens. At Nerd Fitness, we call this the Jar of Awesome, because we are incapable of giving normal names to anything.

Every time we complete an experiment or workout or challenge we're working on, we can add a marble or LEGO piece or widget to the jar. Later, when motivation is low, or we worry about how far we still have to go, we look and see just how far we've already come. This might be enough for us to decide to keep going.

It All Counts

In order to keep doing "the thing," we need to develop the skill of being inconsistently consistent for a long time.

If we can implement any of the ten strategies above, it can tilt the scale slightly in our favor to make us more likely to follow through on our experiment, routine, or habit.

The more times we complete a task, even inconsistently, the more evidence we have that we're capable of completing the task. Over time, these wins accumulate, like marbles in a jar. And at some point, no matter what the voice in our head says, we have definitive proof that lets us say, "I've done this thing a lot of times. Maybe this is just who I am now."

This is how we build momentum. We prove to ourselves we can be different, which builds belief, which creates more momentum, which creates even more belief that we can keep going.

This is my favorite thing to hear about, by the way. I look forward to every email that says, "I don't know how it happened, but I actually *look forward* to exercise now!"

When we pick the right thing that is matched to our personality, when we get over the hump and stay out of the Doom Loop, we have a pretty darn good chance of making the thing part of our life.

Key Insights

Stack wins doing "the thing." Getting an early win, even if it's small, can be the first sign to ourselves that things could be different this time. This means taking a small action and celebrating it. Once we start stacking wins, keep stacking! We can add a small trinket to a jar every time we do the thing, to serve as a motivating reminder of just how far we've already come. We want evidence to show our skeptical selves how much we've already done.

Make "the thing" fun. There are an infinite number of ways to get fit or become productive or make changes. Life is short, so why not find ways to make the thing more fun? Give it a different name, bundle it with another fun activity, invite a friend, or pick a different activity that we actually enjoy.

Make "the thing" beneficial. Every day we do the thing when we don't feel like it, it buys us a day off when we really need it. We can remember that action creates motivation, which creates belief, which creates more action. We can work on our "Big Why" to remind us of how good we're going to feel *after* we have completed what we set out to do.

Make "the thing" necessary. We can use Ulysses Pacts during moments of strength to protect Future Us during times of weakness. We can install app blockers on our phones and website blockers on our computers. We can throw away things that might tempt us later, and use our laziness to our advantage. We can even use money to make a commitment to follow through on something.

Find other people who do "the thing." We become who we spend the most time with. Once we know this, we can choose to spend time with people who do the thing regularly, because we are likely to adopt their behavior. Instead of learning from unrelatable celebrities, we can learn from people who live similar lives and have succeeded how we hope to succeed.

Bring "the thing" closer. The fewer steps between us and the thing, the more likely we are to do the thing regularly. We can hang out at the gym even if we're not ready to work out yet, attend open mics, or carry a book around with us. We're reducing the distance between us and taking action. The opposite can be true too: We can *add* steps between us and the thing we're trying to avoid.

Protect "the thing" with boundaries. Boundaries are the ultimate form of self-care. They're not selfish, they're a sign of self-respect. We need to learn to put on our own oxygen mask before we help others. We can establish boundaries up front to protect our attempt to do the thing, and work to reinforce those boundaries politely but firmly. We can tell people about the rules that we have for saying yes or no to certain things, because people tend to respect rules.

Half-ass "the Thing." We can stop asking, "Do I have time to do the thing?" and instead ask, "How much of the thing do I have time for?" This allows us to constantly adjust the definition of "I did the thing" to fit the chaotic conditions of our unpredictable day. It's not worse or less, just different.

Missed today? Do "the thing" tomorrow. Sometimes we can keep ourselves from going into the Doom Loop before we even notice it, by simply showering tomorrow. A missed day of a routine doesn't need to be a bigger deal than it is. If we can't shower today, shower tomorrow and move on. Being inconsistently consistent is more than okay.

9

WHEN LIFE KICKS YOUR ASS, HERE'S WHAT TO DO

Why hope is the warrior emotion

You may not control all the events that happen to you, but you can decide not to be reduced by them.

—Maya Angelou

In great stories, there's often a shocking plot twist that fundamentally changes everything.

If you're familiar with Joseph Campbell's *The Hero's Journey,* it's referred to as an "Ordeal," which I think totally undersells just how life-changing these can be.

It's Luke watching Darth Vader strike down Obi-Wan in *Star Wars: A New Hope,* or the Avengers watching Thanos snap half of all life in the universe out of existence in *Avengers: Infinity War.* I've run out of contractually allowable mentions of *The Lord of the Rings* for this book, so this is me *not* mentioning that moment when Gandalf fights the Balrog in the Mines of Moria.

Each ordeal results in a "before and after" moment.

Before, when things were okay.

And after, when things are not okay.

We are now at that same "Act Two plot twist" in our own lives.

As the Yiddish proverb reminds us: We plan, God laughs. "Iron Mike" Tyson might have said it even better: "Everybody's got a plan until they get punched in the mouth."

It's a life event in which some part of our identity is taken from us.

It might be a freak injury, a broken leg, or a torn muscle that leaves us bedbound.

It might be a family member's illness that suddenly turns us into a full-time caregiver or a foster parent.

It might be a company-wide downsizing that leaves us jobless and unsure of how we're going to make our mortgage and daycare payments next month.

This is where we need the PACT framework pumped full of the super-soldier serum that transformed Captain America.[27]

I'm going to share some challenging stories in this chapter, most of which do NOT end with "Things got better and they lived happily ever after."

I'm not sharing them to make you say, "Damn, my life could be worse." Everybody is fighting their own battles, and there is no "hierarchy" of devastation. Your challenging situation is valid, regardless of what's happening to somebody else.

I say this because I want you to have these tools in your tool

---

27 I can't believe it took me this long to finally wedge a Captain America reference into the book!

kit for the future. Think of this chapter like the "break glass in case of emergency" device to navigate unexpected experiences or devastations. I hope you never need these tactics, but that's not for me or you to decide.

If you are currently in the middle of your own plot twist, I want to start by saying I'm sorry that life dealt you these crappy cards. I wish I could promise that things will get better.

My younger self, unburdened by any adversity or experience, probably would have made that promise and told you that things "will work out for the best."

I've come to learn, through getting my own ass kicked and spending time with folks who have navigated existential challenges, that making promises like this doesn't help. Telling somebody "I hope things will get better" might make them feel worse, because "better" is neither in their control nor a guarantee.

This is what Kaethe Weingarten, PhD, calls "unreasonable hope," a type of hope "associated with purity and a staunch belief that things will get better because they *should* get better."

Here on earth, in this reality, we need a different playbook.

One that honors and grieves the loss we're feeling, and gives us practical tools for when all hope seems lost.

Give Up Anger

Jodi Ettenberg was a lawyer who never wanted to be a lawyer.

Unlike most people who plan and study to go to law school,

Jodi applied because someone bet her that she couldn't get in. She went to law school at nineteen years old, and while many of her colleagues were strategizing about how to make partner, Jodi was dreaming of traveling the world. So she decided to do something about it.

In 2008, she quit lawyering, started traveling, and created a new identity as a writer who shared her travels through food. Jodi's long-form writing dove into her experiences of various cultures and cuisines through the gluten-free meals that she had to find to keep from getting sick due to celiac disease.

Jodi built a sizable following and turned a one-year sabbatical into her full-time career. She traveled the world, was featured in the media, gave talks at big conferences, and shared her life through her website, Legal Nomads. I even got a chance to share the stage with her once at a conference about community building. She is a delightful human and one of my favorite Canadians.

For a decade, Jodi's new life as a unique food and travel writer remained enjoyable, adventurous, and fulfilling. Her explorations became her identity. One day while cat-sitting for a friend, she had a sudden onset of aggressive medical symptoms that required a trip to the emergency room at a local hospital. After a CT scan, the doctors urged her to let them do a procedure on her spine, called a lumbar puncture or spinal tap, to ensure that she did not have a brain bleed.

And then everything went wrong.

That procedure, for a number of complicated reasons Jodi has shared in her writing, led to a cerebrospinal fluid (CSF) leak that became chronic. Almost immediately, Jodi lost her ability to walk. As she shared in an article she wrote for CNN in 2022:

> My legs were jelly, while at the same time it felt like someone had poured concrete into my lower spine. Within days, I could not stand up. . . . My brain felt like it was sagging in my head, as if it were an anvil pushing down into my neck. When in bed, the room spun. I felt too nauseous to eat and had trouble finding words. My back burned uncontrollably from top to bottom.

Jodi's lifestyle quickly shrank from trekking the entire globe to needing constant care. She had to move back in with her parents in Canada, and could not stand up for more than a few minutes at a time without excruciating pain. She went from a world-traveling nomad eating delicious gluten-free meals to being bedridden. To date, four separate surgical procedures to repair her spine have been unsuccessful, and it's quite likely that Jodi's life will continue on this new path indefinitely, or at least until medicine evolves to find a solution to her chronic leak.

While she is now able to live independently with considerable home care support and accommodations, her world remains very limited. She can stand up for a few hours a day at most.

The more I learned about Jodi's situation, the more my heart broke for her. I wanted to pass along my condolences and my sadness. I wanted to rage at the universe on her behalf. I couldn't believe how unfair all of this was. Furthermore, I had no idea how I could best support her through this.

What I wasn't expecting was for Jodi to have already figured that out.

I candidly asked Jodi how she was able to move forward and not spend every day in a funk. Hell, I spend *lots* of time in a funk, and I'm able-bodied and have more privilege than 99.99 percent of people in history.

She explained how her path from anger to acceptance made all the difference. Early on, she was not only angry at the situation, but also at the people who tried to help:

> Well-meaning people sent me Instagram posts about how positive thinking would help my healing. I read books about happiness, and about how daily affirmations could make me feel better. Yet every word I consumed made me feel more alone.

Life is hard and random. Bad things happen to good people.

Telling somebody with a chronic illness to "look on the bright side" or that "things will get better" is a type of unwelcome toxic positivity. It's toxic because it's corrosive to their feelings.

If we're expected to always look on the bright side, to remain optimistic and to assume things will eventually get better, it minimizes our struggle. It neglects our lived experiences and insults our reality: Things might never get better.

In Gabrielle Zevin's novel *Tomorrow, and Tomorrow, and Tomorrow*, the main character, Sam, shares his frustrations with everybody's naive advice for him on how to behave:

> Throughout his life, Sam had hated being told to "fight," as if sickness were a character failing. Illness could not be defeated, no matter how hard you fought, and pain, once it had you in its grasp, was transformational.

For people like Jodi, life will probably never return to normal. And that is devastating enough. People telling her to just fight harder and stay positive were simply twisting the knife and making her feel even more alone.

Confined to her bed, Jodi searched for a path to process and navigate her new normal. Fortunately, she had attended a ten-day Vipassana meditation course in New Zealand many years prior, where she had learned about acceptance and hatred:

> When you generate hatred or animosity toward your situation, you're the first victim. I have such a limited amount of bandwidth each day, I realized how much of that I was using up on anger. I needed to use that bandwidth for the things that actually mattered. I had to move toward acceptance.

Jodi had to learn to *give up* anger. She only had so much energy, and she chose to stop using that energy toward VERY, *very* understandable anger. Instead she put it toward acceptance. Only after accepting her reality could she move forward with the grieving process. She had to first aknowledge that her world was irrevocably changed, and there's no timeline for processing this:

> Acceptance is a process, not a simple choice. Eventually, it becomes a choice you can make on a daily basis, but to get to that place it first takes a lot of processing, a lot of work, a lot of grief therapy.

As I learned more about Jodi's heroic ability to process her unfair situation that had knocked her down, I couldn't help but think about the Studio Ghibli film *My Neighbors the Yamadas*. The protagonist, Mr. Yamada, gives a speech that hits hard for a children's cartoon:

> Acceptance is the key to surviving the worst situations, without losing heart or breaking up. . . . It's not necessarily bad to resign yourself to a situation. In fact, it's essential. . . . Though it may sound negative, acceptance is the only way out of totally unacceptable situations.

Like Jodi, we can accept with clear eyes and compassion that things aren't okay. We can grieve the paths that might no longer be open to us. Of course, we'll still have days where we get angry at things that are unfair for us moving forward. This is understandable.

After all, processing grief or loss is complex and challenging and could take a long, long time.

However, if we can do the hard work of letting go of our anger, it can free up some much needed mental, spiritual, and emotional bandwidth. It can give us the space to pause and process what's happened, accept our situation, and then decide where our limited energy is best spent each day moving forward.

Declare Expectation Bankruptcy to Avoid Demoralization

I'll return to Jodi's story later in the chapter, but I want to first talk about what we're going to do next after we've gotten our ass kicked.

Once we've paused long enough to process our grief and let go of our anger (which has no specific timeline), we can then see clearly what our new life looks like. One of the most important steps we can take at this point is to remove any unnecessary expectations we might have for how things *should* be (this is "unreasonable hope" again).

We'll do so by embracing a nerdy accounting strategy for running businesses and governments. I promise you this will be liberating, with no math required.

Peter Pyhrr was an accountant working for Texas Instruments in the 1960s. Yes, the company that made the calculator we millennials had to use in high school calculus but really used to play home-brew video games. Pyhrr came up with a new strategy for budgeting that radically transformed many businesses. It was so revolutionary that it led to Pyhrr consulting for the state of Georgia and its governor (and eventual US president) Jimmy Carter on their budgeting.

It's called zero-based budgeting (ZBB).

Let's say each department of a business has a certain budget. And this year, that budget is $1 million, so they spend $1 million. Next year, that department just slaps a 10 percent increase onto its budget and now it's $1.1 million and they will find ways to spend every penny. Each year, this budget grows a bit bigger.

Over time, these budgets and projections become permanent.

The company does things a certain way simply because they've always been done that way. With Pyhrr's ZBB accounting system, instead of starting with the previous year's budget and looking for areas to scrape off some savings, each department starts the year with a budget of zero. They have to then justify why each expense is important for the following year.

Let's set aside whether or not this actually works for governments or large businesses. We're just using it as a framework for our own personal lives, especially after the sh** has hit the fan.

Rather than starting with how life used to be and all the ways we're coming up short, let's preserve our sanity.

ZBB tells us to wipe the slate clean right now. We start at zero and build up from there. We set aside *all* expectations, including the past goals we had for ourselves. We start with a blank slate about future expectations instead of weighing ourselves down with past expectations that are no longer possible.

Let's declare Expectation Bankruptcy.

Today? Right now? This is our reality.

The old normal isn't coming back, possibly ever. We can let go of any obligations outside of our family and what's required to keep us alive. (In chapter 2: Pause, we discussed similar themes, such as doing just enough to stay afloat.)

We can stop asking how we think we should be handling this.

We can say no to obligations (politely).

We can say no to feeling behind.

In addition to declaring Expectation Bankruptcy, we can declare Obligation Bankruptcy and Goal Bankruptcy too. We can be like Steve Carell's character, Michael Scott, in *The Office* and literally yell out loud, "I declare bankruptcy!"

Whatever it is that's weighing us down, we can give ourselves permission to let go. As we're grieving and processing, let's remove anything else that doesn't need to be there. We have enough things on our plate already.

When we suffer an injury, go through a breakup, or process an irrevocable life change, we've found the new baseline: zero. Things are hard enough already; we don't need to *also* put additional pressure or guilt on top of it by retaining the same expectations we used to have.

By shrinking our time frame to "How can I get through this

week?" or even "How can I get through today?" it helps remove additional, unnecessary heartache about grieving or processing the unfairness "the right way."

Today is Day One. We'll deal with tomorrow tomorrow.

Hope IS a Strategy

Instead of "toxic positivity," we're going to practice reasonable hope.

Returning to the work of Weingarten, reasonable hope is a deliberate action, not a feeling. It focuses on what's within our abilities instead of focusing on what we want to happen. It allows for us to exist on a sliding scale between pure hope and pure despair. As we know, there's very little in life that's all-or-nothing.

Weingarten explains that reasonable hope is how we prepare ourselves for whatever comes our way in the future. Author and activist Rebecca Solnit puts it even more bluntly in her book *Hope in the Dark*:

> . . . Hope is not a lottery ticket you can sit on the sofa and clutch, feeling lucky. . . . It is an axe you break down doors with in an emergency. . . .

In many unfortunate situations, developing hope as a skill can be life-preserving.

Enter James Griffith, MD, a professor of psychiatry and

behavioral science at George Washington University's School of Medicine and Health Sciences. He's spent his life developing strategies and conducting research to help patients navigate the complexities of terminal cancer or chronic illness.

Dr. Griffith refers to these strategies as "hope modules," a series of tools to cultivate hope through action when all hope seems lost. Instead of hoping that things turn out for the best, Dr. Griffith treats hope as an active decision to make choices, even when choices are limited.

This type of hope is a strategic decision to accept our current reality and say, "Yes, this is unfair. And here's what I'm capable of doing."

Let's deploy the first hope module: reminding ourselves of who we are, and all the parts of us that make us who we are. These are the personal values or attributes we can anchor ourselves to, even when everything else around has become untethered or parts of our identity have been stolen.

We can start with the parts of our life where our identity remains intact. Where are the parts of ourselves that endure? Although we're dealing with the end of a career or an unexpected illness, there are parts of our lives that endure. Maybe we are still a great parent to our kids, a reliable member of our church group, or a helpful volunteer known for our dependability.

We might be facing frustrating, unfair changes in one part of our life (especially after an injury or illness), but if we look at the totality of our life, it can provide some much needed perspective.

Who we are is much bigger than any one particular part of our identity.

Activating a reminder of all that we are, and highlighting the different things that make us who we are, can be a much needed foundation on which to build our new self. This gives us something real to focus on, instead of only focusing on everything that has been taken from us.

The second hope module asks us to lean on our fellow humans.

This will come as no surprise, but Dr. Griffith's research shows that after a traumatic event or diagnosis, spending time with people we love can help us feel less despair and reduce our stress levels.

It's easy to assume our problems are unique, or that nobody wants to hear them. This is quite common for us people-pleasers, who often don't want to share our feelings for fear of feeling like a burden or appearing weak.

Asking for help is not a sign of weakness.

It's a sign of courage.

This might include asking a trusted friend or family member for support. It might be looking into therapy and getting professional help. It might be picking up the phone for a mental health hotline and being honest that we're not doing well.

The Meaning of Life Is to Find Meaning in Life

In addition to embracing every part of our identity when something is taken from us and leaning on others, we can take deliberate action. After we acknowledge the constraints of our unfair situation, it's now our mission to find meaning in our struggle and actively choose to do *something different.*

The hope module here is referred to as "shift and persist," which comes in two delicious flavors:

"Pathways thinking" asks us to envision a number of different paths still open to us, and then decide to take the next step on one path.

This is most enjoyably demonstrated by our favorite wizard, Gandalf, in *The Fellowship of the Ring.* (I checked with my editor; he let me use one more *Lord of the Rings* reference). Gandalf and the fellowship are lost in the labyrinthian Mines of Moria. They're sitting in front of three identical doors, each leading off to unknown parts of a maze. Befuddled about what to do next, Gandalf finally chooses a path, simply because "the air doesn't smell so foul down there."

We might not need to pick a path while trapped in a mine full of goblins, but we can reduce our despair by identifying the choices in front of us (calling a friend, taking a walk, journaling) and taking the next step on one path.

"Agency thinking" is a reminder to ourselves, when all hope seems lost, that we still have the ability to take action. Even when life has kicked our ass, if we feel trapped, we remind ourselves that our lives are still ours to live.

When we're ready, we can choose to accept our new mission in life: to not just survive from day to day, but to *create meaning.* As the late entrepreneur Peter Barton wrote in his autobiography, *Not Fade Away,* he struggled when a terminal cancer diagnosis stole his life's purpose. As his body was breaking down and his head ached and his spirits were at their lowest, he confided to his wife Laura, "I just don't see the point."

Laura, "as supportive and kind as a person could possibly be," chose defiance on his behalf and replied, "So find one!"

Finding the point became the point.

Pyschologist and Holocaust survivor Viktor Frankl shared a similar sentiment in his book *Man's Search for Meaning*. He explains that our suffering gives us "ample opportunity—even under the most difficult circumstances—to add a deeper meaning to [our] life."

If Frankl can find meaning in Nazi concentration camps, with the most inhumane conditions, then perhaps we can find meaning in our struggle too.

I'm not sharing his words to make you feel bad if you haven't yet found meaning after a loss, diagnosis, or devastation. Instead, I'm saying that when you're ready, there might be more options and pathways open than you realize.

Find a Place to Put Your Love

Aside from Jodi Ettenberg, my other favorite Canadian is a fictional hockey player.

Shoresy, the main character of a TV comedy of the same name, plays senior semipro hockey for the Sudbury Blueberry Bulldogs in Ontario, Canada. Think of *Ted Lasso* on ice, with even more inappropriate jokes, but just as much heart.

In the fourth season of the show, Shoresy has suffered too

many concussions to keep playing hockey. He's trying to figure out what to do with his life after retiring from the game. After thirty-plus years, Shoresy is struggling to navigate a life without the one thing that got him out of bed each morning. He sits down with the owner of the hockey club, Natalie, who shares her own journey with acceptance and mental health after her mom passed away:

> After my mom died, I got a [psychologist]. I gave my mom a lot of love. And my therapist said, "Now that she's gone, you need to find a place to put that love."

Nat decided to put her love into managing the hockey club, helping the local community, and investing in her players. She shares this story with Shoresy, who feels rudderless and is trying to figure out where to put his own time, energy, and efforts for the rest of his life.

He reflects back on a lesson he learned from his love interest on the show:

"If you don't know where to go, go where you're needed."

And this is where Jodi reenters our story.

Jodi's identity as a world-traveling entrepreneur was taken from her. She might never get back the ability to travel outside her city, let alone to another country, ever again. The radius for her once-globetrotting life might remain a small circle around her apartment.

However, like Shoresy, Jodi still has a lot of love to give. Thanks to her ongoing process with acceptance, Jodi has freed up her "brain juice" to put toward a new project.

Jodi found a place to put her love.

She has been elected president of the board of directors for the Spinal CSF Leak Foundation and has given virtual talks to conferences, all from the confines of her bed. She's also coauthored her first research study in the *American Journal of Neuroradiology*. She still publishes gluten-free guides on Legal Nomads, but now she also writes about her health challenges and shares interesting curiosities at JodiEttenberg.com.

I want to make it clear that I'm not saying, "Hey, Jodi did it, and so can you!" I don't know what you are going through, where you're at on your journey, or what life is like for you today.

There's no right way to go through a tragedy, injury, or life-changing event. As Jodi says, this is a process of grieving, learning to let go, and acceptance. By freeing up the space that anger had previously occupied, she was able to find places to put her love, even though it looks completely different from any life path she ever would have expected for herself.

Hope Is the Warrior Emotion

In all the stories above, hope is defined not as a feeling, but a defiant act against the darkness. And as the following story shows, hope might be the only emotion that can help us truly process devastation.

In 2022, musician Nick Cave answered a fan letter written by Valerio, a father who said he was losing faith in people, felt empty and cynical, and worried about passing his feelings on to his son.

I assumed Cave's reply would be something along the lines of "Don't give up hope, stay positive!" Instead, as he explained at his Red Hand Files website, he too grew up "holding the world and the people in it in contempt," but:

> It took a devastation to teach me the preciousness of life and the essential goodness of people. . . . It took a devastation to find hope.

Curious about what the "devastation" was, I started researching and learned that Nick Cave's son Arthur had fallen to his death in 2015 at the age of fifteen. Then his son Jethro passed away in 2022. Losing a child, not to mention two, is the most heartbreaking thing that can happen to a parent.

For Cave, hope needed to be a deliberate choice:

> Unlike cynicism, hopefulness is hard-earned, makes demands upon us, and can often feel like the most indefensible and lonely place on Earth. Hopefulness is not a neutral position. It's adversarial.
>
> It is the warrior emotion that can lay waste to cynicism.

Cave's other definition of hope from his 2022 book *Faith, Hope and Carnage* might be even more powerful:

"Hope is optimism with a broken heart."

When our world falls apart, when life punches us in the gut, when a piece of our identity is taken from us, strategic deployment of hope can keep us from falling into despair.

We can be kind to ourselves, pause and process the pain and the grief we feel.

We can give up anger, and defiantly choose reasonable hope instead.

We can remember all of the parts of our identity, and remember that we still have agency to make choices each day, even when those choices are limited by circumstance.

We can say to ourselves, "Yes, things are not okay and they might not get better. And here's where I'm choosing to put my energy today."

No matter how life has chosen to kick your ass right now, I'm sorry that this happened. I can't know if things will get easier for you. I do know that you're here now, and I'm proud of you for not giving up. When you're ready, I hope you find a place to put your love.

The world needs it now more than ever.

Key Insights

Give up anger. As Jodi explained to me, the more energy we devote to anger, the less energy we have to devote to processing and accepting the hand we've been dealt. If we can give up anger, we have more "brain juice" and bandwidth to start the hard work of grieving and figuring out what comes next.

Declare Expectation Bankruptcy. There's a nerdy type of accounting called Zero-Based Budgeting that starts at zero each year and has to be built from there. Right now, our expectations for the future can begin at zero too. Feel free to loudly yell, "I declare Expectation Bankruptcy!" We have enough on our plate; we don't need to make ourselves feel worse with any past obligations or goals we're no longer able to meet.

Hope is the warrior emotion. Hope is "an axe you break down doors with in an emergency." We're not going to hope that things will get better; we'll cultivate hope that shows we're capable of withstanding ever greater piles of crap headed our way. Hope is an action we take, not something we feel. We can lean on friends or family. We can remember all the different parts of our identity if other parts have been unfairly taken from us. We can narrow our focus to the paths that are still open to us, and remember that we can always make a choice, even if our choices are limited.

Find a place to put your love. As Viktor Frankl explains, the meaning of life is to find the meaning of life for us. When parts of life are taken from us, we still have a wellspring of energy and love that has to go somewhere. The best way to build hope in ourselves is to help others find hope in their own lives. And if we're not sure where to put our love, we can look to *Shoresy*: "If you don't know where to go, go where you're needed."

10

HOW TO NAVIGATE LIFE WITH FLEXIBLE RESILIENCE

Living a PACT Life Year after Year

One can choose to go back toward safety or forward toward growth. Growth must be chosen again and again; fear must be overcome again and again.

—Psychologist Abraham Maslow

We've spent the majority of our journey developing our PACT framework.

I want to zoom out now.

What does life look like following this framework over and over and over? What happens when we apply the steps of Pause, Accept, Change, and Try over months and years? That's when things start to get interesting.

PACT can help us navigate different seasons of life, because life going in unexpected directions is the *only* actual guarantee we can count on. We're going to develop flexible resilience that allows us to make confident adjustments instead of needing a specific plan or working toward a specific outcome.

Instead of seeking *more* control, we're going to make progress by letting go of the need for control.

Here's how we'll get there: We'll start with a comparison between warp-speed spaceships and ancient Polynesian catamarans. We'll then learn to flirt with our future possible selves to explore paths we never thought possible. We'll then embrace happy accidents and leave life open to possibility. And, finally, we'll get comfortable with the unknown.

Why Wayfinding Is Better Than Warp Speed

As we're planning out the rest of our lives, our brains want us to believe we're on a futuristic spaceship with warp-speed capabilities. Because warp speed is unbelievably fast (faster-than-light speed, or FTL), we must be damn sure every tiny detail is perfect in our plan before we hit the big red button.

If we use the wrong coordinates or we're off by a fraction of a degree, we could miss our destination by *light-years*. We might crash into an asteroid field, planet, or a star.

And that would be bad. Personally, I try to avoid crashing into stars at warp speed whenever possible.

The greater, more detailed our life plan, the more perfectly we envision that future, the more rigid our definition of success becomes:

- A yearlong strategy with daily milestones that *should* help us reach our goals.

- A five-year plan that *should* change our lives as long as we execute it perfectly.
- A career path that *should* reward our dedication and give us that prestige we're looking for.

Now, as of the writing of this book, we haven't yet unlocked FTL travel, nor do we have spaceships that can travel at warp speed. Let's also assume that no matter when you read this in the future, we haven't quite figured out teleportation either.

We're thinking about the future with the wrong mindset.

Life is under no obligation to do what we expect, no matter how meticulously we've planned for the future.

We can prove this to ourselves by looking ten years into the past: Did everything turn out the way you expected? You predicted all those world-changing events, right?

Of course not. Nobody did!

I bet you could look back one year ago (or last week maybe) and not have predicted how things turned out.

So, where does this leave us?

Sure, if you want to plan out every month for the next decade, by all means go for it. Sometimes having a big plan with a large goal at the end might help us get started. However, I have a few alternative strategies that might give us a bit more freedom and leave open the door for exciting possibilities.

I know you're intrigued.

We aren't going to plan for perfection.

We're going to prepare for uncertainty.

Instead of working backward from a "dream life," we're going to work outward from where we are today.

We'll do so by becoming Polynesian wayfinders.

Yes, just like in Disney's *Moana*, a movie I have watched with my three-year-old niece (who wants her hair done like "Moana raft hair!") no fewer than fifty times.

Let me first explain "wayfinding," and then I'll dive into why it's an intriguing philosophy for life.

Up until the 1970s, the prevailing theory for how the islands of the South Pacific were settled was "accidental drift." Uneducated Westerners assumed that ancient civilizations, without the aid of maps or compasses, on catamarans made without any modern tools, must have accidentally stumbled across each island in the Pacific.

There was *no way* they could expertly navigate without proper tools, right?

Fortunately, by 1975, modern technology had advanced enough to put the accidental drift theory to the test. Scientists ran sophisticated computer simulations that factored in wind and waves and currents. After sixteen thousand simulations, they discovered not a single simulated voyage was able to "accidentally" make the journey from eastern Polynesia to Hawaii. Not one.

But computer simulations weren't enough. A group of descendants wanted to prove Polynesian wayfinders *could* navigate without any modern technology. And thus, the Polynesian Voyaging Society was formed.

They constructed a catamaran named the *Hōkūle'a*, the first of its kind in nearly six hundred years, without any modern conveniences or tools. And in 1976, the *Hōkūle'a* sailed from Hawaii to Tahiti, a distance of 2,500 miles, without any navigational equipment.[28]

Here's how they did it: They recruited a navigator, Mau Piailug of the Caroline Islands, who had been trained by his father (and his father before him, and so on) in the navigational science of wayfinding.

As navigator Nainoa Thompson explained to author Wade Davis in *The Wayfinders,* wayfinding is much closer to science than it is to art:

> The skills of the traditional navigator are not unlike those of the scientist; one learns through direct experience and the testing of hypotheses, with information drawn from all branches of the natural sciences, astronomy, animal behavior, meteorology, and oceanography.

Piailug knew how the clouds responded to certain incoming weather patterns. He knew that a white tern, a seafaring bird, would always return home to its island at night. Spotting one meant he was within 80 miles (129 km) of landfall and could simply follow the bird back to its home.

On clear nights, he navigated by the location of 220 different stars in the sky; each star during certain hours of the night could be lined up with the horizon. If he couldn't see the stars, he

---

28 In Tahiti, they were greeted like heroes; it was the first time traditional culture had been championed since the mid-1800s, when it was outlawed by colonial administrators.

could stick his leg in the water and feel different ocean currents to guide the ship.

Each morning he could study the color of the sky, the position of the sun, and how the waves moved to help him course-correct the catamaran toward the next island.

Thanks to generous wayfinders like Piailug, this skill has been taught and passed down to future generations. The aforementioned Nainoa Thompson is one of those people, taught by Piailug to navigate the *Hōkūle'a* all over the Pacific. He's now a folk hero in Hawaii for his wayfinding ability, and he has made it his life's work to also pass along these skills to those willing to learn.

Wayfinders have spent their lives internalizing the skills and abilities necessary to calculate their speed and direction from where they sailed; they then use the stars and sun and ocean and animals for guidance, adjusting their course to eventually arrive at their intended target. This style of navigation is also referred to as "dead reckoning": by knowing where we've been and how we got to where we are, we can figure out how to get to where we need to go next.

Rather than having a perfect map and GPS with a specific route to follow, wayfinders know *generally* where they are headed and then leverage their extensive training and context clues to help them navigate more accurately as they get closer.

This is PACT in action!

We can pause and see where we currently are on our journey.

We can accept what life is giving us at the moment: sun, waves, or rain.

We can use context clues to change our strategy.

We can then try to sail in the general direction of our target.

Because we know we can always course-correct if we run into any problems, we have the flexibility to make adjustments along the way. When life throws a storm in our path, we know how to navigate our way back out of it.

To borrow a killer quote from Zen practitioner Jon Kabat-Zinn: "You can't stop the waves, but you can learn how to surf." Or, in our case, sail.

This is Flexible Resilience: making unoptimized progress in an unpredictable world.

Instead of "I will reach this destination by this date," it's making peace with "I will begin my journey in this direction, I know there are different paths available, and I can make changes or course corrections based on what the ocean waves and sky tell me along the way."

What does this look like in practice?

I thought you'd never ask.

Wayfinding as a Life Strategy

Although you might not have aspirations of becoming a writer, I want to share some thoughts on writing that I think actually apply broadly to our lives in true wayfinder fashion.

In her book *Bird by Bird*, author Anne Lamott quotes E. L. Doctorow, who said, "Writing a novel is like driving a car at night. You can see only as far as your headlights, but you can make the whole trip that way."

She continues with further guidance:

> You don't have to see where you're going, you don't have to see your destination or everything you will pass along the way. You just have to see two or three feet ahead of you. This is right up there with the best advice on writing, or life, I have ever heard.

This book you're currently reading is the result of that same wayfinder strategy. I had a rough idea of what I wanted to write: I wanted to help people to try again after failure. I wrote a book proposal (my working title was "Restart"), with an outline and summary and a sample chapter.

I had enough to get started and begin sailing in that direction.

Every few months, the book would take a different turn, and I would follow that new path. I hit a personal storm for about a year that required some repairs and improvements, but kept sailing when possible. Two and a half years later, as I approached my destination, I narrowed my focus and got more specific so that we could reach the end goal: a bookshelf.

You might be wondering, *Steve I'm not a writer, so give me more examples: What does wayfinding look like on a fitness journey?*

I got you covered. It means picking a direction while being

open to changing currents, unexpected outcomes, and learning to navigate stormy weather.

Megan is my favorite success story of the past fifteen years, but not for the reasons you'd expect.

After a few decades of struggling to make consistent progress, she tried a new path that happened to work for her: a new dietary strategy[29] and morning "sassy shuffles" around her neighborhood.

This path worked *unbelievably* well and she lost a considerable amount of weight and dramatically improved her health markers.

And then, in true wayfinder fashion, she took stock of her surroundings and set her sights on a new destination. Instead of asking, "How much weight can I lose?" she asked, "What is my body capable of?"

She started working with Coach Jules Erickson from Nerd Fitness, and they picked a new "island" to sail to: She wanted to build enough strength to do a pull-up, eventually run a 5K, and improve her relationship with food through a more flexible diet. Over the next few years, she hit each of these goals too, falling in love with strength training, running that first 5K, and adding carbs and occasional treats back into her day.

And then she hit a storm.

Needing surgery to remove excess skin due to her weight loss, she ran into multiple complications and *weeks* of reduced

29 Megan decided to follow a low-carb diet, the strategy that allowed her to consume fewer calories. Carbs are now part of her diet! The goal should be to experiment until you find the path that works for you.

movement due to infections and concern over ripped stitches. During this time, to not lose hope, she shifted her direction once again and focused on food, mental health, and light mobility work. Eventually, after her wounds properly healed, she started to exercise again.

Despite these setbacks, Megan's story of persistent resilience didn't go unnoticed. She was featured on the *Today* show, built a large following on Instagram at @Maintaining_Megan, and became an inspiration to people all over the world.

This might be the part where you think, "And Megan lived happily ever after."

But that's not what happened.

Thanks to therapy, Megan recognized some unhealthy patterns around her growing *need to exercise*, a fear of letting people down, and concerns around the increased spotlight on her journey.

So she did something that increased my admiration of her *even more*. She not only took large steps back from training to work on her mental health and relationship with exercise, but she also backed off social media. She's navigated herself through turbulent waters, and is currently parked on an "island" that feels pretty good to her and her family: enjoying her regular job, going on fun family hikes, and very little social media.

Megan also now serves on the board of directors for Girls on the Run Greater Connecticut. This organization helps elementary-aged girls find joy and happiness through running, creating a healthy relationship with exercise no matter their size. This is something Megan wished she had access to as a kid.

Flirt with Your Future Selves

As we're thinking about what comes next in life, we can continue to embrace a wayfinder philosophy.

If the only guarantee is change (especially thanks to modern advances in technology), then a plan is far less important than having the ability to pivot quickly as opportunities come along.

We can start by glancing backward to remind ourselves just how much of life has been a zigzag up until now. As Apple co-founder Steve Jobs said in his 2005 Stanford commencement speech:

> You can't connect the dots looking forward; you can only connect them looking backwards.

Don't worry, I just made myself do fifty burpees for committing the unoriginal sin of quoting Steve Jobs in a book on personal development. I only did so because it's so dang true.

Looking back, it's easy to connect the dots and draw a squiggly line from where we were to where we are now:

- Losing that crappy job that opened the door to the next job that actually fulfilled us.
- Choosing to join that volunteer group that led to a new side-gig opportunity.
- Deciding to swipe right and go to that swing dancing class or out for coffee.

Because we can't know what's coming next, it might feel like we're locked into a pretty permanent path. The reality is that we still have choices, and can decide to zig or zag if something else comes along.

This is best explained in graphic form by author Tim Urban, creator of the site Wait But Why, who has an uncanny ability to create simple drawings to convey complex ideas. Here's his visualization of that Steve Jobs quote made plain:

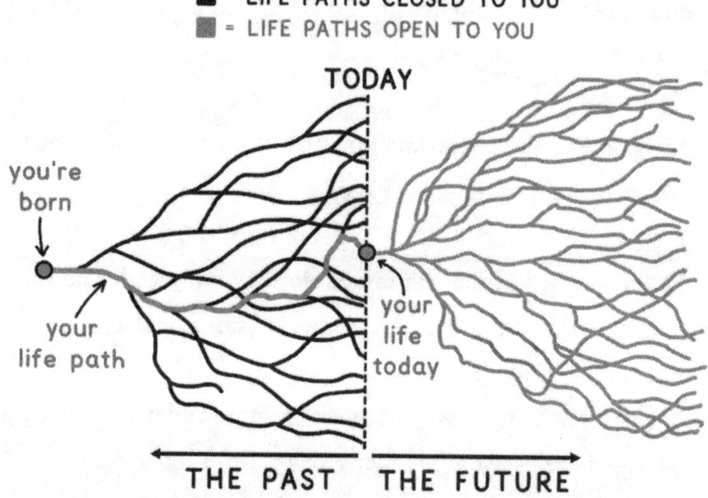

Notice how many paths radiate outward from today.

Infinite universes branch out from each decision or choice.

No matter what path we've followed up until now, it's okay to remind ourselves that we're not locked into any particular life path just because we're already on it. Even if we go all the way through law school and become a lawyer, it doesn't mean we have to be a lawyer forever. That can simply be part of the story that gets us to the next step on our journey.

Exploring widely and trying different paths is almost never a detour or a step backward. This is the entire sentiment covered in David Epstein's book *Range*. While the world demands we specialize and narrow our focus to a single thing (and then stay on that path indefinitely), Epstein provides a compelling argument that we should be doing the opposite.

When we prioritize a variety of skills and experiences and occupations, even when some paths feel like steps backward or detours, they give us the best chance at building a resilient and fulfilling life that can lead to unexpected breakthroughs.

More important, in a world where change is the only constant and entire career paths are disappearing overnight, having transferable skills and lots of general knowledge helps us uncover and capitalize on new or different opportunities.

Put another way, the more "squiggly" our past line is, the more prepared we are for whatever might come our way next. The future is unknowable, particularly with life-changing cultural, technological, environmental, and professional shifts happening with more frequency.

Epstein shares the wisdom of Herminia Ibarra, a professor of organizational behavior at London Business School, who encourages her students to think about their careers as if they're flirting with their possible selves.

Most career counselors advise their students to pick an end

goal of "where do I want to be ten years from now?" and work backward to today to know how to get started.

Ibarra instead encourages her students to start working outward from all the possibilities they have now, just like Tim Urban's drawing:

> It is better to be a scientist of yourself, asking smaller questions that can actually be tested—"Which among my various possible selves should I start to explore now? How can I do that?" Be a flirt with your possible selves.

Interestingly, Ibarra and her students' research reveals that people who jumped to new opportunities, even if these felt like lateral or backward moves, would later report feeling more fulfilled and happier with their decision than those who stayed in the same job. Developing an attitude around exploring widely and flirting with our possible selves can result in more adaptable skills, a wider variety of experiences, and more life enjoyment.

Instead of following a plan, or assuming we must stay on our path, we can navigate life like wayfinders. We can start with where we are right now, and then decide where we'd like to try next, based on what interests us and what doors make themselves available.

The more we keep our eyes open, the less confined we feel to one particular path, the more likely we are to identify which future paths are open to us. That path might look nothing like what we expected, but we can connect the dots, looking backward later.

* * *

Now, I bet you're thinking once again, "Steve, can you give me some real-life examples of people flirting with their possible selves?"

Of course. Meet the eighteenth-century Japanese painter Katsushika Hokusai, most famous for *The Great Wave off Kanagawa* woodblock print. I promise you know this piece of art.

He was known for constantly reinventing himself and changing his art style. He was always flirting with his possible selves and choosing to walk down different paths when they looked interesting. By the time he passed away at age eighty-eight, he had adopted over thirty different artist names, worked with dozens of art styles, and forever changed art and culture throughout the world.

As I was looking for a more modern equivalent of a "possible selves" flirt, I stumbled across the perfect artist. Like Hokusai, she constantly adopted new names and art styles over a career that spanned decades. She just used a different art form to leave her mark.

Meet Loretta Mary Aiken, the original queen of comedy.

As a teenager, Aiken ran away from home after an unspeakably tragic childhood, and began her career as a vaudeville performer on the Chitlin' Circuit. As Anne Cheskey explains in the Asheville *Citizen-Times*, this did not sit well with her brother, who told her that she "was a disgrace to the Aiken name because [she] went on the stage . . . [and] stage women wasn't nothing but prostitutes." So she simply adopted a new stage name—"Jackie Maybley," the name of her previous fiancé—and continued performing.

She eventually found enough success that she moved to New York City, where she flirted with even more possible versions of herself: a writer and a stage performer, part of the Harlem Renaissance.

Another "possible self" she explored was that of a stand-up comedian. She continued to hone her craft, flirting with different personas, and then she found one that stuck: "Moms Mabley."

She realized that if she took out her false teeth, spoke with a raspy voice, and donned the clothing of a grandma, she could get away with exploring more controversial topics without angering her audience, while still sharing important messages.

Her popularity grew and grew, eventually reaching the highest of highs: In 1939, Mabley became the first woman solo act to headline a comedy show at the famous Apollo Theater in Harlem. Over the coming decades, she would continue to flirt with future possible selves and evolve. Chesky continues, in her piece on the comic trailblazer:

> [Her] act became more and more political. White audiences listened. Her accessible and non-threatening persona allowed her to cover topics like ageism, sexuality, gender and racism without alienating her audience.

She would go on to record twenty comedy albums, appear regularly on television shows like *The Ed Sullivan Show*, appear in countless specials, and act in multiple movies. The experimentation never stopped. In her mid-seventies, Mabley became one of the oldest performers ever to have a Top 40 hit with her cover of Dick Holler's "Abraham, Martin and John."

By the time she passed away in 1975, Mabley had trailblazed a comedy path for other women, queer comics, and people of color. By flirting with different selves and personalities and personas, she found the path that worked for her, one that gave her the ability to speak truth to power, and fundamentally change the comedy landscape forever.

If you'll allow me to share one more cool "flirt with your possible selves" story, let's talk about the origins of the award-winning Nashville restaurant Tailor, created by Vivek Surti. Going to dinner at Tailor is an experience, and each step of the process is incredibly *considered.* Surti tells the story of each course in a family-style setting with a menu that's based on Surti's upbringing mixed with his own interests.

After I fell in love with the food, I learned the actual story of how the restaurant came to be. Surti was the son of first-generation Indian immigrants and he ran in my circle of friends at Vanderbilt University. After graduating with a degree in political science, with no professional training or kitchen experience, Surti started flirting with his possible future self as a chef.

He hosted dinner parties at his parents' house, inspired by his mom's Gujarati cuisine. Those parties, and the meals he served, became so popular that he started hosting monthly events at Nashville farmers' markets. Eventually, he created pop-up dinners at various restaurants and event spaces around the city.

This experimental path revealed a more interesting possible self to Surti, so he moved further down that path.

Years later, Surti took all that he had learned and fine-tuned over the years, and partnered with another chef in Nashville, Tandy Wilson, to open a shared restaurant (they each occupied one floor). This went so well that Surti eventually moved into his own restaurant named Tailor, inspired by his grandfather's occupation. Not bad for a political science major with minimal cooking experience.

Be Open to Happy Accidents

Post-it notes run my life. I never would have finished this book without them.

You see, my brain and "remembering things" don't work together well because my head is full of every popular song lyric from the early 2000s.

Post-it notes are on my front door reminding me to take out the trash. They're on my desk reminding me to pay the water bill because for some reason that can't be automated. They're on my fridge reminding me to throw out the leftovers. They're on the counter reminding me to take my medication and telling me which stories go in which chapter.

They're on my computer screen asking me, "Is this a good use of my time?" and reminding me to focus on this book rather than watch another YouTube video about renovating a house on Italy's Amalfi Coast.

Post-it notes are also one of the most famous accidents ever.

Dr. Spencer Silver was a scientist at 3M in the late 1960s, who was researching adhesives in his labs. His goal was to combine various substances and materials to find bigger, tougher, stronger glues. And unfortunately, one experiment resulted in a weak adhesive; it stuck lightly to surfaces but didn't strongly bond to them.

Experiment failed, right?

Many years later, Art Fry, another 3M scientist, was struggling with a frustrating problem: He had little scraps of paper to mark the hymns he was going to sing in church choir, but they kept falling out of his book.

He then remembered Dr. Silver's seminar on his weak adhesive years prior, and realized there was something there. They partnered together and handed out small test pads with the weak glue to everybody at 3M. Employees loved them, and the company began to produce them for consumer use. In another happy accident, the iconic yellow color was because the lab next door only had yellow scrap paper on hand for testing purposes.

Decades later, Post-its have helped millions of people remember to unload the dishwasher or reminded them to pick up the kids after soccer practice. They are also what people wrote on to create the kaleidoscopic "wall of failure" in the Museum of Failure from chapter 1.

You can probably see where this section is headed.

We've spent so much of this book acting like scientists and explorers, so let's not forget that many advancements are a result of accident or happenstance.

Penicillin was accidentally discovered when Alexander Fleming left out a petri dish full of bacteria and it developed a mold that killed the bacteria.

The microwave oven was invented by engineer Percy Spencer when he noticed the chocolate bar in his pocket melted while working with radar magnetrons.

Even recent advancements in diabetes and weight loss medication are downstream of a study conducted on the saliva of the venomous Gila monster.

Here's the important part of each story above: Not only were there interesting accidents, but there was an observant person with an open mind who saw each accident and thought, "I wonder what we can do with this."

This is why we can embrace what landscape artist Bob Ross often explained on his popular television program:[30] "There are no mistakes, only happy accidents."

We can only connect the dots and draw our zigzag line looking backward. We don't know what the future holds, nor can we know the true final result of our experiments and journeys and failures until after the fact.

---

30 There's a heartbreaking documentary about what happened to Bob's business behind the scenes. It's truly an unfortunate situation.

Which means we need to keep our eyes open for whatever comes our way. And not just possibilities, but the lessons we might learn from our (apparent) failures or accidents. Those very "setbacks" or side steps could lead to our next breakthrough:

- Missing our bus could lead to meeting our future spouse who is on the next one.
- Getting fired from one job might free us up for an opportunity that's actually aligned with our skill set.
- Taking a detour at work on a completely unrelated side project that bombs could end up resulting in a new friendship or connection that pays off years down the road.

Life is random and so much of what works or doesn't is out of our hands. All we can do is stay observant as we move down our various paths in life. When unexpected things happen, we can act with curiosity, not judgment.

And we can remember that there are no mistakes, only happy accidents.

Get Comfortable with the Unknown

You might not want to headline at the Apollo nor open a restaurant based on your mom's cooking. You might not want to sail from Tahiti to Hawaii in a catamaran nor have any interest in creating experiments in a laboratory.

That's okay, we can still apply these lessons to our situation. Today is a day to explore lots of possibilities and see what comes of them. We can keep our eyes open to branching paths and happy accidents, because they might end up taking us down a more fulfilling path after all.

To borrow a famous line from Ridley Scott's *Prometheus*: "Big things have small beginnings." Although that quote was uttered by an android talking about the evolution of a face-hugging alien species, we can apply it to our life with much less nefarious expectations.

We don't need to burn the boats, sell our stuff, and go *all in* on a new career.

We don't need to make a big, hairy, audacious goal, nor worry about what we want our perfect life to look like years from now.

We can flirt with our future selves, see which new paths open up, and then lean in to those and see what happens. We can embrace happy accidents and see what lessons or opportunities might come from them.

This is what life looks like when we move from one PACT to another, over and over again. We can learn to not only embrace the unknown, but get excited to learn what's on the other side of it.

Pretty soon, we find ourselves intentionally seeking out discomfort in order to grow.

There's a great quote, often attributed to Joseph Campbell, that I've found encouraging and motivating: "If the path before you is clear, you're probably on somebody else's." In other words, it's beneficial to pick the uncomfortable zigzag that leads to more experiences and growth instead of the comfortable one that makes our world smaller.

We could all probably use a few more squiggly lines when we connect the dots of our life.

If we can get comfortable with sailing into the unknown, amazing things might happen.

Whatever tomorrow brings, we're ready for it.

Not because we expected a specific outcome, but because we were prepared for whatever happens. Even if it's a happy accident.

Key Insights

Wayfinders over warp speed. We don't need the perfect plan for life figured out. We're not a spaceship capable of traveling at warp speed. We can start out with general ideas of where we want to go, and then adjust over time, like Polynesian wayfinders. Instead of making a more detailed plan, we get better at navigating the unknown.

Flirt with your possible selves. At any point, there are multiple possible selves we could become, far more than we realize. And sometimes, making a lateral move or career detour can provide us with the best, most fulfilling experience. With so much of society and the economy changing rapidly, having a career full of interesting experiences and skills will never not be in demand.

Be open to happy accidents. Some of the world's most important discoveries and inventions happened by accident. From penicillin to the microwave to Post-it notes to diabetes medications, surprising outcomes from unexpected accidents or discoveries can change the world. If we believe that there are "no mistakes, only happy accidents," we can keep our eyes open and identify the lesson or opportunity hidden in any setback.

Conclusion

THE END OF THE BEGINNING

Sometimes courage is the quiet voice at the end of the day saying, "I will try again tomorrow."

—Mary Anne Radmacher

On a day when I should have been writing this book, I was browsing Reddit like a good nerd. In between the memes and funny dog videos, I stumbled across a blunt, challenging question about the worst part of being overweight.

The most upvoted answer was as illuminating as it was heartbreaking:

> You put your whole life on hold, telling yourself
> that you will resume living when you lose the weight.
> Then not being consistent with said weight loss journey
> and basically . . . never getting to truly live.

You could write an entire psychology textbook about those two sentences.

This poor person is sharing their deepest frustration, the belief that they can't start living and that they're not "enough" until they reach some arbitrary goal. They avoid photos with their family. They skip certain experiences. They don't date. They decide "I am a failure *until* I reach my goal."

I hope through this book I have convinced you that you are already enough. That you're not a failure simply because something didn't work out in the past. Even if it was your fault or you're not proud of how things went down. Even if you're not as far along on whatever goal you hope will make things better.

You're where you are right now, doing exactly what you need to be doing to qualify as a "human being on planet Earth."

Let's start from a position of "I'm already enough," and then decide how we want to spend the limited free time and energy we have available to us.

We don't need to "optimize" the fun out of everything. We don't need to build and execute a perfect plan. We need to find compassion for ourselves when life goes in an unexpected direction. We can pause, accept, change, try again.

When life feels overwhelming, when we feel behind, we can narrow our focus and just ask, "How can I have a pretty good day today?"

A Hypothetical Day in the PACT Life

Rather than waking up at 5 a.m. because an influencer told us that's the key to optimized wellness, we wake up at 6:47 because our dog licked our face.

While still lying in bed, we decide to check the meme our friend sent us on social media. Rather than immediately feeling "less than" because we're not as successful as the influencers and celebrities we used to follow, we see a cute video of a dog wearing a hat. After a few minutes, we close the app and start our day.

Although we normally make ourselves a protein shake, we don't mind skipping it this morning. Why? Because it's our turn to take the kids out to breakfast, and they want to go to Waffle House. This includes a few choices that still align with our goals, but it also means hash browns, smothered and covered, because they're delicious.

We then drop the kids off at school and head to work.

This month, we're trying a new strategy for organizing our schedule, and it seems to be working so far. When Jan from accounting offers us a doughnut and tells us to "live a little," we explain we have a rule that we "don't eat doughnuts on weekdays." Jan is a real stickler for rules, so rather than pushing back, she nods her head and says, "Maybe I should make a rule like that!"

Lunch is a meal out with coworkers; we already know what we're going to get and how to make it fit within our goals. After work, we hop in the car and drive over to our gym to check out that new class on how to do handstands.

We know we might struggle and look foolish doing these things, but we've embraced the idea that to eventually get good at something, we must first start ugly. We're not afraid to be seen trying, because it's kind of fun to try without expectations, and we want to be a good example for our kids too.

After the gym, we head back home, and accidentally burn the new recipe we're trying for dinner. That's okay, though. We grab the backup meals we already had in the freezer for this very emergency. After dinner, when the kids head off to play video games, we sit down to watch an episode of *The Bear*. We're both in agreement that season 2, episode 7, "Forks" is the greatest episode of TV, possibly of all time.

We talk with our partner about our day and how life will change next week once the summer break starts.

We treaded water during a challenging spring, and we're trying our best to enjoy the time we have together now. We have reasonable hope we can manage whatever surprise pops up tomorrow.

Speaking of surprises, we notice the dog threw up because she ate too much grass while running around outside. Time to get the carpet cleaner.

After cleaning up after our pup, we realize it's time to wind down for bed. We notice the laundry still isn't folded, and some of the kitchen is still messy, but we don't sweat it. We've given ourselves permission to let these things go for now.

It's time to finally get some sleep. We go to our phones to check social media, but all the apps are blocked on our phones after 10 p.m. We jokingly curse Past Us for setting up this Ulysses Pact, but appreciate we can't get sucked back into scrolling through nonsense. We put our phones down, read a few pages in our books, and fall asleep. Not a bad day. Let's see what tomorrow brings.

Make a PACT and See What Happens

We started our book at the end, after a failure.

It only makes sense that we end at the beginning:

A life in which we're much kinder to ourselves when things don't go according to plan.

A life in which we're prepared for the possibility that we might not succeed, because failure is simply one possible outcome of anything worth doing.

A life in which we have a much healthier mindset and realistic expectations of what we're capable of, within the constraints of our delightfully chaotic existence.

Assuming I've done my job right, you've got some reasonable hope moving forward that life will probably get harder, but you will "get good" and be able to handle it.

We know we don't need to succeed with more discipline.

We can fail with more compassion.

We can pause and process what's happening.

We can accept and embrace our humanity.

We can change what experiment we'll conduct next.

We can try again without expectations.

We can confidently ignore the next fad diet, because we're already following a strategy that works for us. We don't mind hearing about yet another influencer who has optimized their morning routine, because we know our life is nothing like theirs.

We have a healthy framework to evaluate the next book we see that promises nirvana and maximum productivity. We can calmly decide which goals and books and experiments we want to try that fit our life, while disregarding the rest.

We win or learn. We accept the happy accidents. We find a way to get good. The failures will pile up, and the complications and the "what the hell just happened" experiences will never stop.

And when it feels like we're starting over, we know we get to bring the knowledge from all previous experiments with us.

With each new change, we learn more about ourselves in the process. We get a bit stronger. No matter what happens, we're free of the expectation that "one true thing" will solve all of our problems. We are aiming to be pretty consistent, most of the time. We know that's enough.

That's a pretty damn great place to be. We have all the tools and the mindset we need to try again. To try again differently. To try again enjoyably.

We can move from experiment to experiment and pre-accept any outcome.

We can tread water for as long as it takes.

We only lose if we stop failing.

Because that means we stopped trying.

Epilogue

WITH A LITTLE HELP FROM MY FRIENDS

All of these lines across my face
Tell you the story of who I am.

—Brandi Carlile, "The Story"

I grew up pretty damn lucky.

Outside of one broken bone, plenty of acne, late puberty, and some bad haircuts, I had no real problems. I lived an idyllic childhood, went to a decent public school, enrolled in a great college, and graduated with manageable student debt. I got my first real job selling construction equipment and very quickly learned I was quite terrible at selling construction equipment.

Shortly after that, I started Nerd Fitness and decided it was going to be my entire identity and life. Inspired by Steve Jobs, I too wanted to put a "dent in the universe." I was motivated by the people who made success their only goal and pushed through pain at all costs to come out on top.

The entrepreneurs who built billion-dollar businesses, the professional athletes with perfectly optimized schedules, the actors with flawless physiques. I fully believed everybody had the same twenty-four hours in the day, and everybody just needed to work harder, "rise and grind," and so on.

I found a tiny bit of success and assumed everybody else should just "do what I do." I declared that we all just needed to be more disciplined and motivated and focused.

Sweet, naive Steve.

The reality was that most of my success was out of my hands. I was born in the right place at the right time, with healthy genetics, to well-off parents, and no chronic health issues. I also had an unhealthy drive to succeed and compete, an addictive personality, a crippling need to be liked, and the good fortune of never having been overweight a day in my life. I have workaholic tendencies and always revert back to "More work and money can solve this problem."

I also was insecure and felt like I had to constantly prove myself and my worth.

Every day was spent grinding for a future payoff that never seemed to arrive. It turned out that I never "made it," simply because I was playing the game of life on the wrong scorecard, with unrealistic expectations and an unsustainable, unhealthy mindset.

I constantly moved the goalposts and perpetually forced myself to push harder. I never allowed myself to feel like I had made it; if I ever had any sort of success, my brain would simply change the rules of the game and compare myself with somebody else who was more successful so that I was once again behind.

And that was before all the turmoil and chaos of the past few years knocked me off my perch. This epilogue is a bit messy, but my life is a bit messy too. It also explains quite a bit of the philosophical journey I've been on over the past five years, so I think maybe that's okay.

Thanks for sticking with me for just a few more pages.

Embracing Wabi-Sabi: Life Is Imperfect, Impermanent, Incomplete

As my life took a few unexpected turns, I realized trying to control everything with an even tighter grip guaranteed that nothing would ever go the way I wanted. Fortunately, I found a much healthier mindset when I stumbled across an ancient Japanese art philosophy.

I know, I know: "Privileged, middle-aged white dude goes through common life challenge and finds meaning in ancient Eastern philosophy" is the most cliché thing of all time, but hear me out.

Wabi-sabi started simply as a preference in the 1500s for locally made art and cookware instead of the fancy-ass tea sets the nobility would import from China. Over the years, this practical decision to "shop local" became popular and took over Japanese tea ceremonies, art, and culture.

It's also a beautiful philosophy that might help anybody trying to better themselves, who gets anxious about not having enough control.

Wabi-sabi asks us to appreciate the beauty in life being imperfect, impermanent, and incomplete.

Unlike many other philosophies or religions that encourage people to pray for certain outcomes or perform rituals to control an uncontrollable world, wabi-sabi does the opposite.

It taught me to embrace the terrifying reality that I have much less control than I want. It taught me that mistakes can be wonderful and nothing is ever "done." It also taught me that nothing lasts forever, no matter how permanent it may seem.

I love that asymmetry and imperfections are revered with wabi-sabi art: weathered wood that highlights its age, cracked bowls and vases repaired in ways to highlight their imperfections, and so on. It's all done to remind us that we too are always changing, and any life well lived will always have scars, cracks, and wrinkles.

It's important that none of this is done in a nihilistic way. Instead, it's to help us enjoy and embrace what we have *now*, but without too tight a grip, precisely because it might be gone tomorrow. It asks us to let go of the expectation that anything must happen a certain way or remain a certain way forever.

It helped me enjoy what's happening *now* and focus my efforts on having a good day *today*. I also don't have expectations that things *should* stay that way tomorrow simply because I *really want them to.*

Yes, as cliché as it sounds, wabi-sabi helped me fall in love with the journey, not the destination.

I used to set specific multiyear plans about where I wanted my business to be and where I wanted my life to be. I wanted to make X amount of dollars, and reach Y level of success. Here's the only thing living with that mindset accomplished: Every day of my life, I felt like I was already behind before I even got out of bed. I wasn't doing enough. I kept telling myself, "But once I get there, then I can slow down and relax." It didn't matter how much success I had, I was always behind and never enough.

I had grand expectations about what needed to be accomplished and how quickly I must get there.

But then the path I had carefully planned for my business fell apart. And then my personal life went down an unexpected path too.

Fortunately, I had spent years embracing and practicing wabi-sabi as a philosophy. Instead of picking an arbitrary big goal for down the road, and constantly feeling behind, I stopped with those expectations and just narrowed my focus:

"How can today be a good day?"

Time spent writing. Time spent doing some form of exercise. Time spent with friends or family. Time spent on an activity that makes me happy. I realized if I could do those things, then that was a pretty good day. It meant I was healthy, I worked on something that fulfilled me, and I got a chance to laugh with my favorite people.

Anything beyond that is a bonus.

I try to have good days more often than not. If I have too many bad days in a row, I pause, accept, decide what needs to change, and then try again tomorrow.

Am I perfect at this? Absolutely not. I drove myself (and my poor editor Pete) crazy trying to write the perfect book. No, seriously. On the one hundredth change I had for the book cover, Pete once called me and jokingly asked a single question: "Do you ever stop tinkering?" It wasn't until I accepted that perfection was a myth that I could finally let this book out into the world.

Also, saying "wabi-sabi" is pretty fun, which has been an added bonus to adopting this philosophy.

It's All for Fun, and It Will Be Okay

In 2015, we hosted our second annual Camp Nerd Fitness. More than three hundred nerds flew in from all over the world to Clayton, Georgia, where we took over a corporate retreat/summer camp.

Our events are full of lovable, anxious, introverted nerds, many of whom traveled alone and are meeting the rest of the community for the first time. As a result, emotions tend to run quite high on the first day.

I stood onstage that opening night and I could see the excitement and anxiety in every camper's eyes. We had already received some pretty stressful news: The weather wasn't going to cooperate that week. Some classes would need to be moved indoors, cutting their attendance caps in half.

Anticipating this, I came up with a quick speech that just flowed out of me:

> Great news, everybody! Something is going to go wrong at this event. I guarantee it. We've planned every detail, but

even that will not be enough. Some classes will be full. We will miss out on something that was great.

This is amazing, because it gives us an opportunity to develop resilience. We'll learn that it's not the end of the world and that we can adapt.

I need everybody to stand up now and repeat after me: "It's all for fun, and it will be okay."

As they all smiled and yelled this in unison, I could see campers' anxiety levels drop. I could watch the relief hit their faces and their shoulders loosen up.

And sure enough, we got absolutely dumped on that week.

We **paused**, **accepted** the weather, and **changed** *every single activity* to be indoors. We **tried** to make it a fun experience: We set up an easel and I drew comically bad portraits of any camper who wanted one. They were *terrible.* But we had fun, and everybody appreciated the levity. Many campers made their cartoon drawings their profile picture on social media for months after.

And then the weather got worse, and we needed another PACT.

We had to shelter in place all together for *hours,* bring every camper to the headquarters, and craft a plan for all campers in case we all had to sleep in the cafeteria. I had to announce to the whole group that all the evening's activities were to be moved inside, we might be getting REAL cozy for the rest of the night, and we didn't know what the future held.

And I was, admittedly, panicking.

But the Nerd Fitness community is full of surprises. While we were trying to reorganize our entire night's plans, campers came up to me saying, "Steve, don't worry! It's all for fun, and it will be okay!" We had a killer party, the weather subsided enough for campers to return to their bunks, and it ended up being my favorite night of the whole week.

That slogan was so memorable that we even had it printed on coffee mugs.

And then, nearly a decade later, life imitated art.

On a particularly challenging day trying to finish this book, my brain exploding with worry, I was drinking coffee out of my "It's all for fun and it will be okay" mug.

Unable to focus and on the verge of freaking out, I walked back to my house in the pouring rain, panicking about the fact that the manuscript wasn't quite where it needed to be. Then the funniest thing happened. I went to close the gate door, and my backpack strap got caught. The backpack slid off my arm, causing me to drop my mug. And sure enough, the mug cracked *perfectly* in two pieces.

Right through the middle of the "It's all for fun, and it will be okay" slogan.

The universe was telling me, "I can't make it any more obvious that things are not okay right now." I stood there in the rain, and let out a giant "Ha-ha!" (like Nelson on *The Simpsons*). The poetic comedy of my life being a mess was symbolized by this broken coffee mug.

Fortunately, I had learned that the imperfections of life are often the very things that show a life well lived. Reading *all the books* on wabi-sabi had started to sink in.

This broken coffee mug was begging me to apply a greater lesson to my struggle.

We humans will also develop chips and cracks. Sometimes we'll get dropped, and we'll break into pieces. That just means we've lived a full life.

And that's when I made a fun decision about what to do with my broken coffee mug. I employed the art of kintsugi (which is very wabi-sabi).

When a bowl or vase is broken, rather than gluing the bowl back together to make it look like it was never broken, artisans combine lacquer with flakes of silver or gold to fill in those cracks, drawing *extra* attention to the imperfections.

By gluing my mug back together with special gold-flecked lacquer, I turned it into a unique piece of art. A true one-of-a-kind original. A piece of pottery that perfectly shows the cracks and flaws and makes it even more special. And for good measure, I decided to practice the art of bonsai by planting a tiny tree in it. I wanted to grow something beautiful out of something broken.

Asking for Help Is a Sign of Strength, Not Weakness

For a long time, I took a lot of pride in never needing to rely on other people.

I believed that this was one of my strengths: figuring everything out on my own. I made myself available to help everybody else, while *never* asking others for help or guidance. I am a conflict-avoidant people pleaser too, so I made sure not to put myself in the uncomfortable position of sharing my struggles.

I certainly didn't want to burden somebody else.

I've come to realize how shortsighted and incorrect this mentality was.

Up until recently, I had spent most of my life on a path that felt certain *and* one that I was in control of. And then that path didn't work out: professionally, personally, and everything in between.

I wrote this book during the most challenging years of my life (so far), and it required me to reframe everything. I didn't realize it, but I had been driving on fumes for a long time, with bald tires and a busted front bumper. My only strategies of *trying harder* and suffering in silence weren't working anymore.

I finally reached out to my friend Sameer to share the news that I was getting divorced and explain I was trying to figure out what my next step was. He instantly replied, "Just come here NOW! We have a guest room and our daughters love you." I spent the next six weeks living with Sameer and his wife, Megan (both of whom I've known since the first day of college!), and their two lovely daughters who call me "Stevo."

I then visited my brother Jack and his wife, Meagan, and their daughter who calls me "Unka Steve." Next, it was off to visit my parents and sister in Massachusetts. If I'm being honest, waking up in my childhood bed felt like giant steps backward in the game of life, especially for a divorced forty-year-old man. Fortunately, I had done a lot of work and had compassion for myself, and I knew this was a new chapter in a (hopefully) long book. I was appreciative that I had so many people who cared about me and who were willing to help me navigate a tough time.

I have more privilege than most—no kids (yet)—and even I needed a village to help keep me afloat through the past two years. I'm not sure you'd be reading this without the support of my friends and family.

When I was in the depths of despair trying to push this book across the finish line, my friend Tim Grahl made a comment that I hadn't even considered:

"Don't you have lots of friends who are really good at organizing book structure? Ask them for help!" I told him I didn't want to be a bother, and that I just needed to struggle through it *a bit more.* Sure, I had *already* been struggling for eight months on the structure alone, and I thought the correct solution was "struggle more, but *harder.*" Fortunately, Tim convinced me.

I texted Josh Kaufman, author of *The Personal MBA*, and asked if I could come visit because I needed help. Forty-eight hours later, Josh was cooking me dinner in his beautiful house, while his son and I played *Elden Ring.*

Later that night, Josh sat down with my ugly manuscript, and a few hours later had carved away the parts of the book that didn't fit. He threw away all the parts where I was trying to write like other authors and kept the parts that were "Maximum Steve."

The following week, I finally had the courage to share the draft with some other trusted friends, and I started to feel less shame and less alone about the problems I was facing.

I felt like Steve Rogers at the end of *Avengers: Endgame.* That amazing moment when all the Avengers assemble and the entire Wakandan army (I just did the hand signal) shows up to help him fight Thanos.

I finally allowed myself to believe that asking for help wasn't a weakness or a burden, but something that showed courage.

I realize now that no matter how much we think we're self-made, we all still stand on the shoulders of the amazing people around us. My friends and family and community and coworkers helped pick me up and helped me push this project across the finish line.

Next Time Is Next Time; Now Is Now

In the novel *Tom Lake*, Ann Patchett tells the story of Lara Kenison, a mom of three who has lived a life of adventure and interacted with famous people over the decades. As she recounts her life to her grown daughters, she remembers one summer spent on the shores of Tom Lake as a performer in *Our Town*. During one such performance, a fellow performer had a medical emergency and missed the show, and passed away shortly thereafter.

> "Was that his last performance?" Nell asks. "That night with you?"
>
> Funny how we never know. Uncle Wallace didn't go onstage thinking it would be his last night. When my last night came, I didn't know it either, my last time to play Emily, my last swim in the lake.

I was reminded of this idea of "the last time" when I discovered another concept:

"Ichi-go, ichi-e," which translates to "one time, one meeting."

No matter how many times we've done something, or how many times we hang out with somebody, it's never been done exactly that same way. Each encounter, no matter how routine, is actually the first and only time it'll ever happen that way. Keeping this in mind encourages us to slow down, be present, and enjoy what's happening in front of us.

As somebody who is always living for "what's next," slowing down and being present has proven more difficult than any workout or physical feat I've attempted.

It's also changed me as a person, and I'm very appreciative that it has. It certainly made all the difference in my final interactions with my grandmother.

A few years ago, my gramma presented my brother, sister, and me with three of her favorite handmade quilts. Because I live in Nashville, I was given the log cabin quilt. She said:

> I was going to have these gifted to you grandkids after I passed away, but I want to give them to you now so that we can enjoy this moment together.

She carefully explained why she gave us a particular quilt, and what the story was behind its creation. It was one of those "I will never forget this" moments, one I'm glad I shared with my gramma rather than hearing about it after her passing.

Fast forward to 2024; with my personal life starting over, and knowing Gramma (now ninety-four years old) was slowing down, I got a chance to visit her throughout the summer. I embraced "ichi-go, ichi-e" and remembered the words of Ann Patchett, knowing that each time with her might be the last.

As I was putting the finishing touches on this book, Gramma Barbara Kamb passed away peacefully at the age of ninety-five. I'm glad I had the chance to know more about her life story over the past few years and to be present for each visit. I saw her the day before she passed, kissed her on the forehead, and said good-bye. Although I'm glad I had that opportunity, I also had already been saying good-bye to her with each visit.

I now find myself at the start of a new journey, one whose path is a question mark. I don't know what my future holds, but I feel okay not knowing. For the first time in a long time, I'm focused on having a good day today. We'll deal with tomorrow tomorrow.

Thank you for reading.

It means the world to me.

—Steve Kamb, Nashville, Tennessee

NEXT STEPS AND RESOURCES

To quote Andy Dufresne at the end of *The Shawshank Redemption*, "If you've come this far, maybe you're willing to come a little further . . ."

Here are a few steps you can take next, when you're ready.

You would be my hero if you left an honest review of this book on the online platform of your choice: Amazon, Goodreads, and so on! Reviews help fellow readers decide if they're willing to take a chance on a book, something that's in ever-smaller supply these days. Besides, humans helping humans is swell—thanks!

Please share this book with a friend who you think might benefit from knowing they're not alone with their challenges.

I write a weekly newsletter about trying again and living a nerdy and fulfilling life at SteveKamb.com. I've been writing it for seventeen-plus years and it's my favorite thing I do each week. If you enjoyed this book then I know you'll enjoy my short weekly email.

This book was made possible by hundreds of books,

articles, studies, and conversations. If you want to explore those sources, check out **HowToTryAgain.com/sources** for all the details for each chapter, links to the books, and resources.

Don't forget to check out the "wall of failure" at How To TryAgain.com/fail and please add your own. It can be cathartic to realize that your failures aren't particularly that unique. Besides, they make you part of the least exclusive club on the planet: humanity.

And, one last time . . . thank you for being here, thank you for being you, and thank you for taking the time to read my book.

GLOSSARY OF FUN TERMS

This book is full of fun (and not-so-fun) terms that help explain what's going on in our brains and our lives. When we can put names to them and point out what's happening, it gives us the best chance to implement change (or forgive ourselves for changing at a slower, more sustainable pace).

Each term or phrase also has the corresponding chapter number where it's first addressed.

Are you playing on the right scorecard? (chapter 6): We often grade ourselves on a scorecard that isn't our own, and compare our success to somebody else who is playing life on a different scorecard entirely. This is how we get in trouble. Instead of asking "Is the juice worth the squeeze?" we should be asking "Do I even want juice?"

"Back to normal" fallacy (chapter 3): When we assume some magical, predictable "normal" life is hiding just around the corner. We lie to ourselves that next week "things will get back to normal," instead of accepting the chaos that is our life right now. For most of us, there IS no normal. *That's normal.*

"Be curious, not judgmental" (chapter 4): A quote from the TV show *Ted Lasso* incorrectly attributed to Walt Whitman, though the sentiment is well taken. We can embrace our thoughts or our past behaviors with curiosity. They already happened. Judging them doesn't help. Instead, we can ask why things happened the way they did, and see if we can apply any lessons for future changes.

Build your own buffet plate (chapter 6): Every day, we're bombarded with people telling us about the "one true way" to get healthy or happy. Many of these strategies contradict one another. Think of these things like a cruise ship buffet plate. Put the food on our plate that works for us, without worrying what somebody else's plate looks like.

Dead reckoning (chapter 10): By knowing where we've been, and how we got here, we can use context clues to decide where we need to go next. This also works for life: We can take all of our past experiences and decide where to go from here.

Doom Loop (chapter 7): Where "all or nothing" becomes "all, then nothing." It's a never-ending loop of feeling "less than" (step 1), then getting overly excited that the next thing will solve all our problems (step 2), going all in for a time (step 3), and then giving up when life gets in the way (step 4), falling right back into feeling "less than."

Expectation Bankruptcy (chapter 9): When life feels so unfair or we are dealing with so much crap that we allow ourselves to declare bankruptcy for any future goal, social obligation, or experience we might feel like we need to have. This gives us permission to just focus on surviving the next day or the next week without feeling guilty for not doing more.

Find a place to put your love (chapter 9): From the television show *Shoresy*; when we're struggling in life, it can sometimes help to give our love to somebody else or another cause. That same episode provides guidance for when we don't know where we should help: "If you don't know where to go, go where you're needed."

"Five Whys" method (chapter 4): A method made famous by Taiichi Ohno of the Toyota corporation: Asking "why" five times seems to be the sweet spot for getting down to the root of a problem, whether it's an assembly line of Japanese cars or why we skipped our workout yesterday.

Flirt with your possible selves (chapter 10): Instead of teaching her students to ask, "Where do I want to be ten years from now?" Professor Herminia Ibarra encourages them to start working outward from all the possibilities they have now: "Which among my various possible selves should I explore?" Be a flirt! We can find ways to "try out" different selves and then commit to a path once we know what works.

Get good ("git gud") (chapter 5): Made famous by *Dark Souls* fans, reminding us that doing hard things can be fun and rewarding, even if we struggle. It's a reminder that we can improve our skills, and that is going to teach us a lot about ourselves.

Hofstadter's Law (chapter 7): Coined by author Douglas Hofstadter, this law states: No matter what you're doing, it will always take longer than you expect, even when you take into account

Hofstadter's Law. If this is the case, we might choose to pick more sustainable changes that don't make us miserable.

"Ichi-go, ichi-e" (epilogue): A Japanese saying that translates to "one time, one meeting." No matter how many times we've done something, or how many times we hang out with people, it's never been done exactly that same way.

Invisible scripts (chapter 6): A term popularized by author Ramit Sethi, these are the hidden rules, philosophies, beliefs, and behaviors that govern our decision making. They're often passed down by our parents or taught to us by society. We need to ask if these rules and beliefs are still serving us.

"It's all for fun and it will be okay" (epilogue): The phrase I uttered while onstage at Camp Nerd Fitness before everything went wrong and we still had fun. Life will not go according to plan, and things will *not* be okay. We can decide that's okay. Not because things will magically get better, but because we'll have the resilience to weather whatever storm comes in.

Jar of Awesome (chapter 8): A term we use at Nerd Fitness to help people remind themselves of their progress. Every time you complete the task you're working on, add a marble or LEGO to a jar. The goal is to keep putting more "wins" in the jar.

Notice and name (chapter 7): Our brains are weird, and we can interrupt the patterns that we fall into by noticing and naming them when they happen. This puts distance between us and the thoughts, giving us a chance to pause and decide if the thought is worth paying attention to.

Pre-accept any outcome (chapter 5): A term shared with me by performance coach Josh Nichols about letting go of expectations. Putting *more* pressure on our goals or *needing* a certain outcome is the fastest path to ensure it never happens. By pre-accepting any outcome, we get out of our own head, and just focus on the experiment itself.

Premortem (chapter 7): Before we embark on a project, experiment, or goal, we can imagine what *will* go wrong. The goal is to literally identify all of the potential pitfalls, or why the thing won't work. Paradoxically, focusing on the worst-case scenario can often make us feel better because we now feel prepared and know how to handle it when it comes.

Reasonable hope (chapter 9): As described by Kaethe Weingarten, PhD, it's looking at hope as a practice that accepts the future is open, uncertain, and influenceable. At the same time, it acknowledges there are very real contextual and sociocultural factors. In other words, "This might suck, and here's what I can do in my small sphere of influence."

Self-compassion (chapter 7): As defined by Kristin Neff, PhD, it's "doing a U-turn and giving yourself the same compassion you'd naturally show a friend when you're struggling or feeling badly about yourself. It means being supportive when you're facing a life challenge, feel inadequate, or make a mistake."

Self-efficacy (chapter 8): This is a term coined by psychologist Albert Bandura that means "belief in ourselves to make positive change in our lives." When we have mastery experiences (proof we've done "the thing" or something like it in the past), when we see a friend do it, and when we are in a good mental place, these things can improve our self-belief.

Shower tomorrow (chapter 8): A missed day of a routine

doesn't need to be a bigger deal than it is. If we can't shower today because life happened, who cares?! We shower tomorrow and move on. If we bring this same mentality to missed workouts or other routines, it can keep us out of the Doom Loop before our brains even notice.

Square One doesn't exist (chapter 1): We know this as the beginning. But we stand on the shoulders of our Past Us and bring all of that hard-earned knowledge with us. This can help us avoid the same pitfalls or making the same mistakes, and make it a few steps further this next time. Even when we start over, it's never back at the beginning.

Start ugly (chapter 5): A book by David duChemin about the creative process, and also a killer motto for life. It's so easy to put pressure on ourselves to perform well immediately. The only way to go from suck to not-suck is to be okay launching our first experiment out into the void. Feel free to pretend it's just a test run for next time. We can just try things.

Temptation bundling (chapter 8): When we combine our goal activity with something that's fun and do both at the same time to *make the activity more fun.* For example: Take a daily walk while listening to a favorite podcast. Walk on the treadmill while watching a favorite reality TV show. This is why I floss my teeth in the shower.

Thoughts think themselves (chapter 7): To put some distance between ourselves and those thoughts (especially the critical ones), let's give our thoughts a name. Perhaps his name is Chaz, we met on Craigslist, he has a ferret named Sparky, and he rents the room upstairs. We can choose which of Chaz's thoughts are worth listening to and which ones should be ignored.

Toxic positivity (chapter 9): A cousin of unreasonable hope (see below). It's when you tell somebody who's struggling to "look on the bright side" and "try affirmations" and "things will get better! I know it!" For many, they don't get better, so this is just making them feel more alone with their struggle.

Tread water (chapter 2): To confidently do the bare minimum to stay afloat in our lives for months or years. We can tread water with our workouts (do one exercise), or with our diet (eating one healthy meal), or with any other part of our life. The goal is to preserve energy and brainpower for as long as necessary until we can start swimming in the right direction again.

Ulysses Pact (chapter 8): When we take action during a moment of strength to protect Future Us from going off track during times of weakness. More specifically, this can mean setting up conditions now (throwing away certain foods, blocking time-wasting apps, and so on), setting up future conditions where we can't possibly get distracted or make a wrong decision because it's overwhelmingly difficult compared to just doing the right thing.

Unreasonable hope (chapter 9): A term coined by clinical psychologist Kaethe Weingarten, PhD, "associated with purity and a staunch belief that things will get better because they *should* get better."

Wabi-sabi (epilogue): Japanese Zen philosophy built around an appreciation of the fact that life is imperfect, impermanent, and incomplete. If perfection is unattainable, if we never get to be done, and nothing lasts forever, then we might as well get to work embracing today.

Wayfinding (chapter 10): The art of seafaring navigation by Polynesian wayfinders was without maps or compasses. They used techniques to settle thousands of square miles of tiny islands. They used the stars, ocean currents, knowledge of certain bird migration patterns, and weather patterns. Instead of needing exact coordinates to sail to (or a ten-year plan), wayfinding is when we have a rough idea and we're open to changing based on conditions, rather than rushing.

"Yes, and" philosophy (chapter 3): Built on the principles of improv comedy and Dialectical Behavioral Therapy (DBT), "Yes, and" embraces the paradoxes of life. It's accepting two things to be true at the same time. "Yes! Things absolutely suck right now, AND here's what I'm able to do today."

Zoom In, Zoom Out (chapter 4): When we conduct an experiment, we need to set the parameters, and then pick a date four to six weeks in the future and put it on our calendar. We can then zoom in and focus on just doing the work every day. And then, four to six weeks later, we can zoom out, evaluate the experiment, and decide if it's still worth doing.

ACKNOWLEDGMENTS

Life is a team sport. So is writing a book.

This one took more than I ever would have expected.

To my editor Pete Wolverton, thanks for your patience and helping me find the 70,000 words of great stuff amid 150,000 words of chaos. And thanks to the St. Martin's Press team!

To my agent David Fugate, thanks for politely telling me my first idea for this book wasn't very good and going all in on this one.

To the incredible coaches and my coworkers at Team Nerd Fitness, thank you for taking care of our nerds and inspiring a lot of the lessons in this book. To the Nerd Fitness Rebellion, thank you for sticking with me for seventeen years and counting. Rebellions are built on hope, and I'm going to do my best to make sure you always feel welcome and excited to be part of our Rebellion.

Thanks to Josh Kaufman, who dropped everything he was doing on a moment's notice to help me cut out all the parts where I wasn't confident in my own voice, and instead found the parts that embraced "Maximum Steve." Tell Nathan to keep the controller ready for me.

Thanks to Tim Grahl, who helped change this book's trajectory with a series of three short conversations spread across a few quick weeks. I don't want to know where it would have ended up otherwise.

Thanks to Adam Baker (have we turned the corner yet?), Eric Ruiz, and Matt Myers, who helped read drafts of this book and provided me with honest and direct feedback wrapped with care.

Thanks to the Nerdlings (Jodi Ettenberg and Mike Sowden) for being a sounding board throughout the year, and providing book feedback, and keeping me sane on the internet.

Thanks to Sameer and Morg of House Morgupta for helping me stay afloat, and hi to Clara and Sofia. Thanks to the Vanderbilt BoT for endless hours of humor and distraction. Anchor down!

A huge thanks to Mike Shade and Eli Strait and the *Chasing Scratch* Velcren, online and in real life. This community is something special. #LGLG.

Thanks to Ramit Sethi for being a great friend, constant source of guidance in life and business, and always being available to provide advice when I need it.

Thanks to Chris Guillebeau for being an inspiration first, then a friend and mentor, and a gaming buddy recently.

Thanks to James Clear for your hospitality, 10-plus years of friendship, and showing me how to market a book enjoyably.

Shout-out to the rest of the Sedona (and NYC) crew: Mark Manson, Nir Eyal, Shane Parrish, Ryan Holiday, Eric Barker, Tim Urban, David Epstein, Ali Abdaal, and Derek Thompson, all of who helped me in one way or another get out of my own way and get back to writing.

Thanks, Jack Rahaim, for your very old-man wisdom, our conversations, and always keeping me on my toes. Thanks to the fine folks at Honest Coffee, 8th and Roast, Radish, and Thai Ni Yom, for caffeinating and fueling me to get this across the finish line.

And finally, thank you to my family.

To Jack and Fieldy, Coco, Sushi, and George, thanks for letting me visit for far longer than any houseguest should stay. Thanks to my mom (Ma!) and dad (D!) and my sister Emily (Emmy!) for always being cheerleaders of my work, and helping me navigate more chaos than normal.

This book is dedicated to my gramma Barbara Kamb. I hope I made you proud.

ABOUT THE AUTHOR

Mackenzie LaRoe

Steve Kamb is an author and the founder of Nerd Fitness. Since 2009, he's helped busy people get stronger, live healthier, and build heroic habits. He's published a thousand articles backed by scientific research and full of nerdy references that have been read by tens of millions of people to level up their lives. Kamb writes a weekly newsletter at SteveKamb.com, which is read by 100,000+ superhumans. He currently resides in Nashville, Tennessee, where he plays golf decently and music poorly.